To a Lovely Lady —

Many thanks for all your help and understanding. Your thoughts and prayers have proven to me that you truley have put your hand in the hands of the man. I consider it an honor to call you friend! Take care of Glenn — He's a special "pussycat" also.

Always

Harry Waters

Wouldn't Take Nothin' for My Journey Now

Wouldn't Take Nothin' for My Journey Now

JOCK LAUTERER

The University of North Carolina Press *Chapel Hill*

ISBN 0-8078-1330-3

Library of Congress Catalog Card Number 80-13425

Library of Congress Cataloging in Publication Data

Lauterer, Jock.
Wouldn't take nothin' for my journey now.

1. Aged—North Carolina—Pictorial works.
I. Title.
HQ1064.U6N494   305.2'6'09756   80-13425
ISBN 0-8078-1330-3

To my grandmothers:

Lena Sloop Dellinger, 90

Lionne Adsit Rush, 95

Contents

Preface

During my years as cofounder and coeditor of a weekly newspaper in Rutherford County, North Carolina, I was afforded the unique opportunity of roaming through the countryside, meeting, photographing, and interviewing a very special generation of Americans—the last that vividly recalls a folk past. The members of that generation were born before the turn of the century and grew up without cars, televisions, telephones, highways, shopping centers, and all the trappings of the twentieth century. Instead they were nurtured by strong families, a cohesive community life, and a set of values fast becoming obsolete in today's society.

In the ten years that I have been in the hills of North Carolina I have come into contact with literally hundreds of these amazing folk—and folk they are. In the literal sense. They possess unsung skills passed down from their elders, strong beliefs, and an undergirding faith in their fellow man which is all but disappearing from more urban societies. In southwestern North Carolina, and in Rutherford County specifically, I found a strain of old people who are truly remnants of a vanishing human landscape.

Here in the hills are aged rockmasons, violin makers, blacksmiths, molasses makers, chairmakers, retired railroad men, gold miners, and country doctors. Old Joe Millard, the blacksmith; Cotton-head Joe, the honorary mayor of Harris Station; John Bynum Bubba-Lee Walker Junior, the town character of Ellenboro; or old Big John Moore, the pig man of Frog Level—these people are true to their natures; they shy at any publicity and are the last to acknowledge their exemplary traits and skills in the vanishing folk arts of the southern highlands.

These people are a living legacy of inestimable value. Their memories and craftsmanship span two centuries, and they lucidly recall a land of farms, a land where the small, single-family farm was dominant, a land where time passed slowly, and a land peopled by hardy, self-sufficient, proud, confident countryfolk.

Skilled old people like these can probably be found all over the nation. But in this state, in Appalachia, the customs and life-styles are better preserved—manifesting themselves in the marvelous people portrayed in these pages. They provide a bridge to the past, a vast library of oral history that supplies the seeker with volumes of human information on what it was like to be alive in the early 1900s. They are valuable as living historians. Unfortunately they and their knowledge are by and large taken for granted. So when they are gone, a chapter of personal history is irretrievably lost. Most of the subjects were at the time of the interviews in their eighties, at least. At this writing well over half have died. A bit of old Appalachia, the Old South, and, indeed, America dies with the unrecorded passing of each of these people.

I believe that their wisdom and values matter to us "moderns," and that belief drives me to record their stories, to show their sincere, handsomely lined faces, and to share their resilient zest for life. These portraits are a storehouse of recollections, wisdom, and practical knowledge from the goodly people who give North Carolina and the South its deeply rooted folk heritage.

I attempted to make these interviews simple and informal. I came as a new friend rather than as a reporter. Since I was an editor of the local newspaper, my real mission was plain and I never felt that I was deluding anyone. I used a notepad—not a tape recorder—and I took pictures only during the latter stages of the interviews. In many instances the interview became a conversation, the new friend became a real friend, and that visit became just the first of many visits.

I must thank several people who have helped me and stood close during the writing of this book. Maggie Palmer Lauterer, my wife, best friend, and creative companion, has encouraged me, year after year, to continue this effort. She is the primary reason that this material has reached publication in book form. Also, I must thank my former partners at *This Week* in Forest City, Ron Paris and Bill Blair, who were so supportive of my work, and my typesetter and manuscript typist, Billie Faulkner, who was a constant source of good humor and hard work. I must also mention my friends at The University of North Carolina Press, Malcolm Call, editor in chief, Pat Evans, special assistant to the editor, and David Perry, my editor—all of whom I can never thank enough for believing in this project from the very beginning.

Jock Lauterer

Introduction

Rutherford County did not know a four-lane highway or a shopping mall until the last decade. The mountains held time in check, at least for a while. The guardian hills to the west and north presented an obstacle to westward-moving pioneers, who found easier passage through the mountains along the broad Catawba Valley. Rutherford became a quiet backwater. The main road of the nineteenth century was the Lincoln Turnpike, which wound from the east, across the county, to the peaks of Rumbling Bald, a sheer rock face that quaked enough to earn its name. The modern highways followed the old wagon traces, but still Rutherford remained relatively isolated through the 1960s.

The county can be visualized by cupping the left hand into a "C" and placing it on the palm of the right hand. The cupped hand represents the crescent of mountains to the west, north, and northeast. These protect the played-out cotton lands and leafy watersheds that lie in the gently undulating foothills, creased by creeks and rivers.

This area was primarily farmland, but here, as elsewhere, the small farm has long been in decline. Since the turn of the century cotton milling has been important. Today the textile mills are as busy as ever, and other industries have moved in, including furniture plants, an automotive reconditioning trade, and various factories turning out products from plastic molds.

In the 1970s the "grand isolation" of Rutherford began to change. A major highway was built from Shelby to Rutherfordton, and traffic flowed through to the resorts and ski slopes of the higher mountains to the north.

The county has only three real towns. Forest City, the farthest east, is the largest. The residents abandoned its original name of Burnt Chimney around the turn of the century when they felt that the name was not in keeping with the spirit of progress. Spindale, the next town to the west, is a milltown, but one bursting with civic pride. Rutherfordton, the county seat and farthest west, is the oldest of the three but smallest in population. It is a historic village and prides itself in its gracious neighborhoods, well-kept older houses, and active support of the arts. These towns lie close together in a ten-mile stretch, and their borders are now indefinable to the newcomer.

Around the three towns sprawl the smaller communities of Rutherford County—Bostic, Westminster, Sunshine, Golden Valley, Gilkey, Union Mills, Harris, Shiloh, Green Hill, Henrietta, Caroleen, Cliffside, Ellenboro, Hollis, Duncan's Creek, Hopewell, Logan, and Shingle Hollow.

It takes just under thirty seconds for the big transport trucks to roll through the typical Rutherford County community of Westminster—past the old church, up the grade past the truck stop, past the old school, past Long's Store, past Clayton Norville's decaying but still grand machine shop, and past the back-to-back road sign that modestly proclaims this patch of land Westminster. Five generations of Longs, Andrews, Carsons, and Watsons have lived there.

Some came from Lancaster County, Pennsylvania, by way of the Shenandoah Valley, crossing the James River on rafts and moving south in Conestoga wagons in the spring of 1735

until they reached the fertile wilderness of Cane Creek Valley.

"There was another bunch of them who came down from the Pittsburg area after Braddock took quite a beating from the Indians," related seventy-five-year-old Gilmer Long. The new settlers were mostly of English descent, and a few were Germans.

They founded New Britain, the oldest settlement in the county. Later, one of Gilmer's relatives, Colonel William Long, who was a friend of George Washington, moved here to land granted him by the king for service in the French and Indian War. The family named the community Westminster to remind them of their English homeland. Long donated seven acres for a church, and a log church, Britain Presbyterian, was built in 1768. After the Revolution local residents discreetly changed the name of the church to Brittain to distinguish it from the warring mother country.

During the Revolution, Westminster contributed more than its share to the rebel side. The commander of the forces from Rutherford County at the Battle of Kings Mountain was Andrew Hampton, who lived near Westminster. Lieutenant Thomas McCullough was mortally wounded in that battle and was buried at Brittain Church. Major Patric Watson, Captain John Watson, Captain James S. Withrow, and Brigadier Major John Moore—all revolutionary soldiers—were also buried there.

Brittain Presbyterian Church is the oldest church west of the Catawba and probably the state's second oldest church. It has had three buildings; the present one was built in 1852 out of hand-dressed local lumber and bricked over in 1940. The church graveyard contains hundreds of prerevolutionary markers, some illegible, some barely readable, and some marked only by a simple stone slab with no inscription. Soldiers from the Revolution, the Civil War, the Spanish-American War, and the First and Second World Wars are plainly marked.

The buildings that formed Westminster School now serve as homes. The campus, which included about fourteen acres, was donated in 1901 by four families, the Longs, Weeks, Hamptons, and Morrises. "I was a mere child," recalled Gilmer. "Reverend R. C. Morrison was spending the day with us after church. They got to talking about good schooling for the local boys, and Papa said he'd like to see a good high school built and started that very afternoon with his contribution. Then my uncle joined in, and in a very short time they got the presbytery interested in it. Then in the fall of 1901 it opened."

An administration building built out of locally made brick was erected on the campus, along with a two-story building that housed classrooms and dormitory rooms for the girls. Three cottages were built as dormitories for the boys.

Gilmer, who was five, started at the school with his seven-year-old sister. They walked the mile from their home to school and paid a six-dollar monthly tuition. Eventually he took courses in Latin, algebra, geometry, trigonometry, German, Greek, Bible, chemistry, and physics. At its peak, the school had some four hundred students enrolled.

When the county schools consolidated in the early twenties, the end was in sight for Westminster School, and in 1924 the school closed its doors. Gilmer now lives in one of the former boys' cottages on the grounds of the school he attended in his boyhood. "These public schools don't give you the training that we got here," he said.

The brick administration building is gone today, and the other two boys' cottages are vacant. The big classroom and dormitory building, the top floor now removed, has been made into

apartments. In back scrub pines choke the old athletic field. Across the highway, Mrs. Cleter Yelton lives in the covered pump house for the school.

Zalph Clements's grocery and feed store looks as though it is about to fall in. The old store sits on a dirt road just off the main highway. When the school was big and cotton was king, Zalph Clements's place was a thriving country store. But not now. The supports are buckling, and the old Coca-Cola signs are rusted and bullet riddled. Broken windows face the world. Briars choke the doorway.

Clayton Norville passed away in the fall of 1971. His machine shop stands as a sort of tribute, full of his inventions and mechanical contraptions. When he died he was still active as a gunsmith, machinist, surveyor, blacksmith, and inventor.

He and his two sons, Harvey and James, ran a cotton gin for forty years in back of the shop. The sons are now in the cattle business, but they keep the shop the way their father left it. One of their prized momentos of their father is his handmade surveyor's transit. He etched all three hundred and sixty degree marks on a lathe. For cross hairs for the telescope he used a spider web. He hand-tooled the aluminum frame and whittled the wooden tripod. "I don't know why he built all these things," said Harvey. "It would have been less trouble for him to have bought a tractor. But I guess he just got it in his head he wanted to do it."

Clayton's passing marks the end of an era in Westminster. With him goes the gin, the machine shop, and the days of the old academy. In his lifetime the hard-surfaced road and electricity arrived. His sons are the sons of the sons of pioneers. The original families are dwindling out. Westminster has seen its heyday. Local folks doubt that it will grow much. Brittain Church, historic and still very much alive, will doubtless persist, but as Harvey says, "There's a change that's taking place—and there's nothing you can do about it but go with it."

Ernest and Edna Murphy

Ernest and Edna Murphy lived on a farmstead that was perched on a knoll overlooking Cedar Creek. The only way to their house was a log footbridge sixty feet long and ten inches wide. Their forty acres included the most idyllic swimming, tubing, and picnicking spot in the area.

Ernest rented out tables for fifty cents, and the swimming was free. They liked it like that and didn't mind the people. "We like having folks come around, just so long as they're polite and don't run off with things like the fishermen did. Carried off what they pleased outa my barn." Ernest removed a yellow billed cap to reveal a snowy thatch of thick hair, which he rubbed pleasurably. "Don't allow no fishermen no more," he said firmly.

On the hottest day of the year, it was relatively cool on Cedar Creek, an icy stream that tumbles out of the northwest Rutherford County hill country near Youngs Peak and Roanhorse Mountain. Still, it was hot enough for one of their chickens to keel over. "Had to bury him," Edna said, lamenting the loss of a laying hen.

Bury a perfectly good dinner? How come?

"Lord, Boy," Edna hooted, "if I'm gonna eat chicken I wanna ring their necks myself! I don't want to eat no dead chicken!"

Ernest, sitting in front of the fan after a day spent "'mater pickin'," chuckled. "But that's the onliest kind to eat—*dead* chickens."

"Lord," she vowed, "if I had all the hog stuff, things I've canned and handled, and chickens I've wrung in my time—why they'd be a pile as big as this house."

Whoops and splashes sounded noisily from below the Murphy house where the footlog crossed broad, shallow Cedar Creek. "Swimmers," Edna said, nodding her head crowned by plaited silver braids in the direction of the sounds. "I never heard so much squealin', squawkin', hollerin', and cryin'."

The Murphys lived a simple, if not Spartan, existence—a life-style common to small-farm life fifty years ago. Ernest was eighty and Edna was almost that, yet they insisted on living like they always had—simple and hard. "We come up hard and we know what hard work is. And we raised up six boys hard. And in a way *good* too," Edna insisted. "I made their clothes—other than their overalls. Knit their wool socks and long underwear. They wanted to put 'em in welfare clothes, but we wouldn't hear of it. Why, they didn't look too fancy but they *was* dressed warm—and et good."

She baked their bread each day, fed the chickens, gathered the eggs, milked the cow, made her own butter, tended to the house, and cooked on a woodstove no matter how hot it was. Ernest picked tomatoes, plowed with a mule in the garden, tended the stock, ground his own cornmeal, and ran his blacksmith shop when he needed to. They heated with wood, and their boys, now grown men, helped keep the woodshed packed with stovewood.

They had lived there fifty-six years. "Ain't been livin' here. Just campin'," Ernest joked. The house had been in the family ever since Ernest's Uncle Sim Murphy built it at the base of Roanhorse Mountain in 1889. Next, Edna's grandpa, Rile Searcy, had it.

Edna, who came to live with "Grandpa and Grandma" when she was just thirteen, recalled the flood of 1916 that inundated the valley and washed away the road that used to run in front of the house. "The water came right up to the front yard, but stopped there. It filled this valley clear up." Edna shook her head grimly. "Hogs, drownded people, houses, and logs went over these shoals. Seems like it rained forever. The water went from this yard clear over to them big gum trees yonder side of the valley. Hit was a pitiful lookin' time.

"My youngest brother liked to have got drownded. He got caught trying to wade across. The current got him and washed him away, but he just caught a branch as he went by and pulled hisself out. We all just battled it out and did the best we could."

The flood eventually washed away the underpinnings of the wheat mill, but the corn mill, built during slavery down on the creek, escaped the flood. In time, it too fell in, and all that remained were the rock pilings and the massive millstones.

"I'll give 'em away to anyone who can carry 'em off." Again that sparkle of mischief in Ernest's eyes. "I mean *carry* 'em off—under their arms, not have 'em hauled off, but *carried* off," Ernest said, pleased with his joke.

The interior of the house was walled with heart pine, honey-toned by time. The chimney was a sure-standing piece of masonry which was put together with red mud, now chipped and pockmarked by home-building mud daubers. Ernest bragged on the fireplace's draw. "I tell folks when I put on my socks in the morning, I have to hold on to 'em, or else the draw'll jerk 'em up the chimney."

The Murphys, who didn't have a car, gave in to the advances of the twentieth century only grudgingly. They had a phone, but Ernest scowled, "Yu' got a phone, then everybody knows yer business." They had two televisions, but as Ernest said, "One got sound and no picture, and the other's got picture and no sound."

"Most folks watch the TV but that ain't *my* hobby," Edna said with disdain. "I never could do that. I guess I just don't have time. I'm allus workin'."

They raised six boys on the creek. "And ain't nary of 'em drownded," Ernest attested. Five of the six were in the service, but when they called

the youngest, Edna said, grinning, "Ernest told 'em, 'Just take me instead!'"

The Murphys not only killed and cured their own meat, but they had their own family customs about just how to do things. They made their own sausage and cooked it down for thirty minutes. Edna called this "wiltin' it down." Then they buried this and the "middlin' meat" in ashes in the smokehouse. Ernest insisted this preserved the meat perfectly, "since there ain't no bug alive that can get around in ashes. He spins his wheels."

Like most old farms the Murphy place had a system of outbuildings, each one designed to fill a specific need. There was a chicken coop, wash-house, smokehouse, toolshed, woodshed, black-smith shop, cornmeal millshed, potato house, livestock barn, corncrib, and hog pen.

Ernest tromped from one to the other, tending and tinkering with various things—something he liked to do after a hard day working. He picked up a curious-looking piece of machinery and waggled it experimentally. "Betcha don't know what *that* is. Why it's a T-model valve grinder," he informed.

He walked on to the cornmeal mill, where a chicken nested in a burnt-out woodstove, past the well-used woodshed, and then to the blacksmith shop. There he had tacked all manner of metal doodads in some order known only to him. Ernest placed a bent mule shoe on the anvil in the center of the shop and began to beat it with a hammer while he talked.

"They tell you old people had a hard time. But old people got the best in the country. Did you know that? Those *were* the good times. A man could go visit the neighbor for two weeks. But now, taxes and the cost of running a farm . . ." He held aloft for inspection the mule shoe. Then he pointed to the various gewgaws hanging rusted on the walls—things he'd fashioned himself from iron. "See, I ain't got no money. I have to make things for myself." He wasn't complaining—it was a proud statement of fact. He held up a sling-blade made from a handsaw blade. "And hit'll cut too, buddy," he said.

About that time Edna came by carrying two tin pails, on her way to do the milking. Ernest fell in step behind her, and they strolled along the path to the barn. The jersey cow came at a trot and entered her stall, where she waited patiently. Edna sat on the stool and began the milking. The sound of fresh milk thrumming a froth in the pail made a noise like a five-stroke roll on a snare drum.

On the other side of the barn Ernest fed and inspected Kate and Ethel, the mules. Kate was a big creature that Ernest plainly adored. "She's seventy-nine and I'm eighty," he grinned. Displaying his two-year-old, he said, "This one I'm gonna break and raise so I can ride to deer hunt on her. That's Ethel. See, the deer won't pay her no 'tention."

Next he checked on his mud-wallowing, seven-hundred-pound hog. "Fatten a hog on nothin' but corn if'n y'want him to grow. Don' use none of them suppliments," he said. "They don't taste right."

In the back of the house a rock-faced spring bubbled from underneath a towering beech tree. Ernest dipped a generous gourd of water from the pool. "Drink from the gourd, and hit'll keep you from having sugar diabetes, I allus heard. Anyhow, I never been bothered by it." He offered the gourd and then drank in his turn.

Back from milking, Edna propped her arms on her hips and surveyed Ernest, still grimy from picking, but grinning anyhow. "Y'know, he works like a slave, don' he?" Edna half-scolded.

Ernest proudly shot back, "Hard work's good for you. You can eat anything you want to—and you go right to sleep."

6

George Robertson

George Robertson lived on the Bostic highway near Sunshine. He was eighty-seven, but he still worked his yard and land as he had always done. "Farmed all my life," he said. "Ain't been nary a year but I farmed."

His family had tilled the same property for four generations. "I was born down in that cabin yonder," he said, walking toward the log cabin across the field. "Ain't no telling how old that house is, but I'd guess it's near two hundred years old. I was born down there. 1884. The last of eleven of us. Never lived nowhere else. Farmed

the whole time." Pausing for breath, he gazed out from beneath a felt hat, hands crossed across his chest.

He reached the cabin and patted its still sturdy side. The hand-hewn logs were twelve to fourteen inches wide and notched at the corners in half-

dovetail style. Vines straggled out of the gaping doorway and windows, but the building itself was intact.

George was quiet for a time—remembering. "Oh, Lordy," he began, "I remember there was apple, peach, and cherry trees around here.

9

Place used to be covered up with fruit trees. Yonder's the one tree still standing. We made our living on the farm. Never had to buy anything—except coffee and sugar. Used to cut and dry fruit in rainy weather. Took our flour down to Rastus Smart's brother's rolling mill in Shelby and got it ground."

His bushy white eyebrows knotted. "Had a sister die in childbirth. Then one of my brothers died of lockjaw. He stepped on a nail. Didn't have doctors around much back at that time. Then there was a fever that come that killed near about fifteen to twenty people in the community. Mother died of it, too. J. W. Biggerstaff's whole family died within a month of it—except the old man. He weathered through. That was 1897. I'll never forget that year. '97."

He started back up the dirt road, carefully measuring his steps over the rutted field. "Oh, we had some good times. I remember J. P. D. Withrow's Big Days over in Hollis t'other side of the mountain. Wasn't but about four miles over there," he said casually, acknowledging that he had walked the entire length of Cherry Mountain just to get to the celebration.

"I was there the last time they had a Big Day—I don't remember what year it was—when they had a murder. And that's what stopped it. Levi Thomas got in an argument with a feller named Lige Hunt. Levi shot him—right there in the crowd. I remember hearing that shot. Lige Hunt's boy went home and got a gun and come back to kill Levi. So they took Levi and locked him in a room 'til the law could get there. After that year they never had another Big Day."

Robertson stopped again to examine his lands. Prickly cockleburs clung to his patched woolen pants. He picked them off unconcernedly, adding, "Not many people's left who's been to those Big Days. J. P. D. Withrow always put on a big spread. Food for everybody—every Thanksgiving and on July 4th. I never missed one."

Stopping by the big weatherboarded house by the road, he observed, "We moved up here when I was about eleven." He nodded toward the highway. "That road out there, it was nothing but a muddy hole. Took two hours by wagon to get to Bostic. I hauled many a load of cross ties to Bostic. Two trips a day and got eight cents a stick. Could carry eight at a time, so that's what? Sixty-four cents a day?

"And we never got paid in money. Had to trade it out at one of the stores up here in town. I guess those store fellers really had it on us. And it would be axle deep in mud many a time. Now that's a fact," he said, noting a truck whizzing effortlessly down the grade toward Bostic, a bare seven minutes over the hill.

He turned and walked back up the road, leaving the log cabin down in the hollow and the old two-story frame house of his childhood. Crossing the highway, he labored up his front yard to sit on the front wall by his modest white house. "Why, we used to be able to buy three large plugs of chewing tobacco for twenty-five cents. That's quite a difference from now."

He stared at the harvest of new acorns sending their shoots earthward at his feet. "I'm still telling people around here yet," the old man said half to himself. "I still say, I loved that kind of time we had then. I really enjoyed it. Those old kinds of living we had."

Nettie Frady

Deep in the hollow of a woody glen far out in the Bill's Creek Community, a weathered farmhouse snuggled like a sleeping cat in the lap of the green-aproned mountains. And on the porch of the little house sat two women, mother and daughter. With knees together and hands folded in the laps of their long dresses, they craned their heads expectantly to see who was coming down their road. For no one came down that road who wasn't coming to see Estelle Bailey and her mother, Aunt Nettie Frady.

The road ended there, after winding around the lee side of the hill and curling to a stop beneath the big buckeye and silver maple trees that shaded the house in the front. "I planted that tree of a seed myself," seventy-four-year-old Estelle said proudly, pointing to the maple. The relatives and visitors sitting about on the cool porch on this Sunday afternoon raised their eyes respectfully to the big tree and nodded, the younger ones trying to comprehend.

Like that old maple, Aunt Nettie also carried her years well. "How old you reckon I am?" she enjoyed teasing her guests. They always guessed low, which tickled Aunt Nettie. "I'm ninety-four," she announced. A face as wrinkled as a used napkin wrinkled even more in a delighted smile, and her eyes shone at the porch-full of devotees who had come to pay homage to the grand old woman of Bill's Creek.

On that Sunday afternoon the porch was more crowded than a watermelon stand on the third of July. Folks sat around in cane-bottom chairs and talked of old times. Aunt Nettie had been a midwife in the Bill's Creek region. She recalled one time when "the baby came feet-foremost. We had a real time, but the babe was fine." And she added, "I only charged five dollars to birth a child."

Under the porch a rooster strutted and a hen cackled about. Old Jeff the dog snoozed, stretched out flat on the foot-worn porch steps, head between his paws.

One of the visitors pointed and asked about a sawed-off limb from the big maple. Estelle told the story, looking at the tree as if she could see it all happening again. "That branch it upped and died, and I asked my son Floyd to come saw it off. And when he did, it fell on the wash-house. We plumb forgot about that," she laughed.

"I used to hang Grady's wristwatch on the branch and go to scrubbin' so's I could tell when it was time to commence cooking supper. Well, I had an old scrub board, and I'd scrub and beat and boil 'em . . ."

"Why, Law', yes!" exclaimed neighbor Annie Hill, sitting beside her.

Estelle went on. "We'd have to beat, beat, beat 'em on the battin' block and then boil them clothes and then put 'em out in the sunshine to dry—and then they smelled so sunshiney good. Then when washing machines come out, I said to myself, how can that thing wash clothes? It don't boil 'em!"

Everybody on the porch rocked back and enjoyed that one. Annie picked up the conversation. "They still call wash day Blue Monday. Why, if they see'd what we had to do, they'd called it Black Monday!"

Aunt Nettie rose slowly from her chair on the porch and headed for the steps in a slow but steady walk. "Goin' to get the eggs," she confided to the congregation on the porch. Inside the bottom of a special bushel basket under the porch steps two brown eggs were deposited. Aunt Nettie scooped them up and just as slowly made her way back up the steps to the porch and into the kitchen.

"Isn't it just wonderful the way she gets around—at her age," one of the visitors admired. That got them talking about bursitis and arthritis troubles, which seemed to be just about every-

body's burden. "Oh, them 'Ritus brothers," Estelle exclaimed, knitting her forehead in mock fury. "If I could put them in a sack and pour gas on 'em, I'd burn 'em up. They're so mean," she glowered.

"Well," said Annie, making light her pains, "I have to contend with Arthur."

The talk and laughter on the shady porch ebbed and surged, punctuated now and again by a pleasant silence. Not an embarrassed silence in which all were trying to think madly of something to say but just a quiet spell in which they listened, watched, and quietly appreciated each other's presence.

On the weathered board walls hung a sign reading "God Bless This Home," an RC Cola thermometer, a fishing net, and a chain whittled from poplar by Estelle's late husband, Roy.

Someone in the state government had six months before unearthed some twenty thousand medals that had been made in 1919 to honor North Carolina veterans of the First World War. For some reason they had been packed away and forgotten. Now Estelle had received the medal intended for her husband.

She clasped it with both hands and said, "I wish't Roy could have been alive to get this medal, but somehow I think he knows." Roy Bailey had been gone for two years. "You can't imagine what it's like to miss a companion like that," Estelle said frankly. "I told myself I'd never sow another garden again. But as time goes on, life just goes along, so I've started to sow again. The crib's fallin' down so I wanted a new tin roof on it to keep it from rottin'. My son didn't understand, but he did like I asked. I just wanted to keep the farm the way Roy had it."

Now, for no apparent reason and without any cue, Aunt Nettie began singing. She took leave of the crowd on the porch and stared off across the hollow as she sang, loudly and clearly, "Oh, how I'd love to hear my mother pray again . . ." She beat the time with her hands on her apron lap, and she didn't miss a note.

She ended the song and blushed, "Oh, I'll hush up," but changed her mind and began, "Oh, can you say you're ready, . . . ready, brothers, . . . ready for the soul's bright home . . ."

Her voice was still strong, full of the character and richness of her years. "Whew," she grinned happily after that song, patting her heart. "Can't sing like I used to. Used to be when I could get to church I couldn't wait for the choir to go to singin'," and then she was off into another old gospel song. "Cheerrr-uppp my bru-ther, walk in the sunshine, we'll understand it all by and by . . ."

By this time, other members of the porch clan were joining in. Annie took up the alto, someone added a tentative bass, and even Estelle tried a note or two. It sounded fine, singing like that for no one in particular and everyone in general. And there was Aunt Nettie, beating out the time with her hands, a rapt expression on her face as she sat and gazed into the sky, ". . . all by and by."

Next came "I don't want to cross Jordan alone . . . ," and there was a sad story to be told. Aunt Nettie said after the song, "My first husband was a good Christian man, but when he lay a-dyin', I just couldn't stand it and I went out into the yard. I could see he's a-goin' and a-goin' fast. But he hollered, 'Nettie come back in here and sing,' so I sang his favorite song, 'I don't want to cross Jordan alone,' and he took my hand and sang with me. But he could only get out the first couple of words, poor feller. He was a good Christian man."

Long shadows stretched from the maple shading the porch. The friends and visitors began drifting away, saying their goodbyes. Annie gave

Aunt Nettie a long hug and told her, "I hope you have many more days, and I hope they're happy ones." And she replied, "I love you." Then, turning to the others standing there, she said, "I love you all."

Aunt Nettie's visitors got in their cars and turned around, one by one, and the caravan moved slowly up the twining road through the hollow to the main road. Aunt Nettie and Estelle watched them go. The ninety-four-year-old grand dame of Bill's Creek said, partly to herself and partly to the departed, "Good friends is good friends."

John Bright

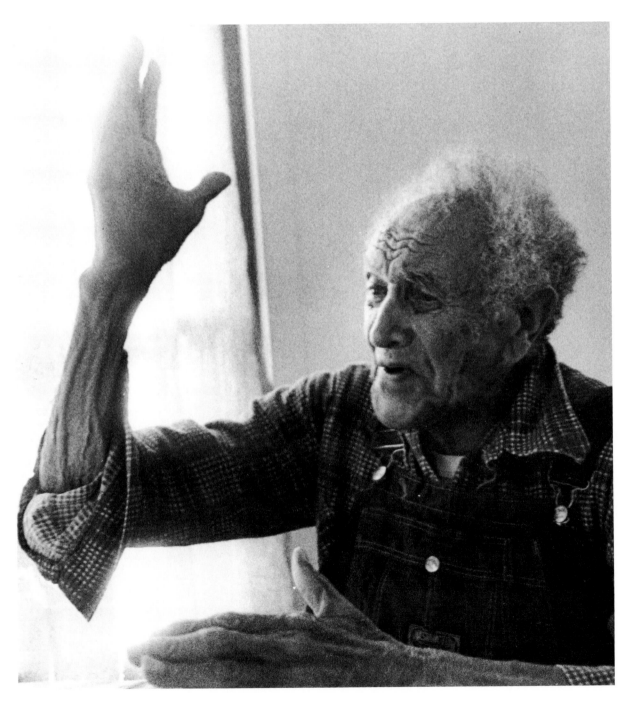

"Bright in name—but not in knowledge," ninety-five-year-old John Bright recited his homemade introduction. "Born stupid and uneducated and all like that." But John's legacy was just the opposite. The unschooled son of a slave, he and his wife Lollie, sent all six of their children through college.

A dirt farmer for all of his life, John lived with his youngest daughter in a comfortable brick home she had built for them near Gray's Chapel on County Line Road west of Rutherfordton.

Sitting peacefully with head in hands or with those gnarled copper hands folded calmly across his overalls, the white-haired man remembered without rancor. "My daddy was born a slave. Back then folks were born and sold and driven around everywhere. A man named Bright bought him away from his family when he was only five years old. Took him up around Mun'ferd Cove. My daddy, he tol' me he remembered he had to walk alongside Mr. Bright up there on his big horse and Mr. Bright would reach down and strike my daddy on the ankles to keep him from getting too close to the horse.

"My daddy was seven years old when those men came through—they called 'em Yankees. Daddy tol' me they'd catch a man's good stout mule or horse and never say nuthin' about it and jus' go on and leave you—even if you cussed and cried. Sech as that went on, y'know. Well, my daddy was freed but he stayed on and worked for Mr. Bright. Called him 'my ol' boss.' My daddy didn't know nuthin' about his people. Didn't have no name. His 'ol' boss' just called him Henry, and then gave him his name, Bright.

"On the day he died Daddy told me, he said, 'Son, be straight and honest. If you owe anybody, go pay 'em. If you can't, then go see 'em.' That's what Daddy said. That's the best education there is. Be straight and honest."

John's father farmed all around western Rutherford County. When "Ol' Boss" died, he tenant farmed with his former master's two unmarried daughters, "Miz Polly and Miz Dinah." Henry Bright called them "my ol' mizzes." John recalled his daddy would finish a year tenant farming and "didn't have five cents clear money." So he bought a mountain place "nobody else wouldn't have" near Whitehouse, where John was born in 1883.

He was raised a farm boy and learned all there was about mules and plowing, planting, and harvesting. "I been on the farm all of my days," John said. "I wudn't no big-time farmer, but I seen it done, and I done hoed and chopped and sweated and plowed. Now they've got tractors," he frowned with contempt. "They can work the crop and *never even touch the ground.*

"Back then we plowed with a mule and a single-foot. Lord, pulling a crosscut saw for ten hours for sixty cents a day. That's haaard livin'. Payin' rent, fertilizer—whew, that's hard go. Why, landlords said they makin' nuthin', and the farmer shore wudn't makin' nuthin'. So sounds like nobody was makin' nuthin' at all. Lord, it was a lonesome time."

In 1910 he married Lollie Lynch. "My children don't let me use this word, but Law', my father-in-law, he was what they used to call a big nigger, a big farmer. Me 'n Lollie got married in April of nineteen and ten. She's an ol' time *good* country woman. She taught in a rural school for a while until they passed some law and said she was unqualified."

He remembered some things that are distant history to younger generations. The big flood of 1916 that devastated Western North Carolina, he refers to as "the Big Wash-Out." Raising both gaunt arms over his head, he said, "It was the sixteenth day of July, nineteen and sixteen. We were living at the old Doc Birch Twitty farm. I got up on a Sunday and went to the door and

hollered, 'Lollie come see, the water's plumb up over Mr. Nanney's lot fence.' It stopped before it got to our house, but there was mountains slidin' into the river further up. And people lost and never heard of again. That's just how lonesome it was."

The Brights began to raise a family, and their children seemed to have a natural drive for learning. "I never know'd children that wanted to learn so bad. The little fellers would go out and get mud to make letters out. I said, 'Look here, Lollie. Lookit them pore lil fellers taking mud and makin' their A-B-C's.'"

They decided that they would have to move to the city to get their children a proper education. So in 1935 they went to Greensboro. But the big city was just too much for John. "City life—whooo!" he whooped. "There was automobiles, *boo boo boo*, and traffic a-goin' *boo boo boo*. All a-goin' twenty-four hours a day. I said, that's not for me. I'd rather be off in a quiet place. Why, I *had*.

"And besides, I had worked all my days on the farm. I didn't know how to do nuthin' in town. I couldn't do a thing but plow the mule, and they didn't have no mules in Greensboro. So I come

19

on home and farmed and shipped the family fruits and canned food and every kind of thing that'd grow and tried to send 'em something and provide for 'em so they could be educated.

"My wife stayed down there. Now, she's been a hustler. She's *straight*. She tol' me, 'John, there ain't a woman in Greensboro can beat me.' An' that's right!" he declared with a flash of pride.

He was able to joke about sacrificing his marriage for the sake of his children's education. "We get along all right. For a year at a time we wudn't have a cross word. . . . Well, I guess we don't have a cross word—I don't see her!" he grinned.

Serious again, he leaned closer. "You've seen these people who come from the backwoods to the city and they let the city run away with them. You know, they fall among the lowest type of people. But our children, they retained their virtue, because my wife, she runs the house. That's why I'm so thankful. They got their education and they've got enough knowledge now to know how to appreciate what they've got. I thought they could not have a better thing on earth than that."

He proudly listed his children's accomplishments: Janie Sue Bright finished at Winston-Salem Teacher's College, became a teacher in Maryland, and was now retired; Chester L. Bright, a graduate of A. and T. State University, taught and later served as an agricultural extension agent in Beaufort County, North Carolina, and was now retired; Jean M. Bright graduated and taught at A. and T. State University, studied at Columbia University, Atlanta University, and the University of North Carolina at Chapel Hill, and was now retired; Mildren B. Payton graduated from A. and T., continued her studies at Cornell and Southern Illinois University, received her law degree from North

Carolina Central University, where she taught law, and taught at Appalachian State University; John W. Bright, Jr., studied at A. and T., and was now an assistant supervisor of electronics at the U.S. Census Bureau at Suitland, Maryland; Sarah B. Smyre, the youngest, graduated from A. and T., took her master's degree from New York University, and had been teaching for thirty years, twenty of those in Greensboro.

John's grandson Louis, who also went to A. and T., liked to visit the eight-acre family farm in Rutherford County and work. "He wants to plant an orchard," he said in open admiration. "He don't care how hard and rough the work is. He wants me to help him. He's just an ol'-time country child, I reckon. He don't dread going out and trying to *get it*."

Running a hand roughly back and forth through his bushy white hair, he looked out across the land that swooped steeply away from the new house, and it was as if he could see all the way to the big cities where his progeny were working and prospering. John didn't have to follow a mule any more or send canned vegetables to his struggling young scholars. "The children have done well, and I feel good about it. And in my foolish way of thinking it was the Lord's doing. My Lollie always said, 'John, the Lord helps anybody who helps himself.' Oh, she didn't mind telling me."

Quintenna Boone Hampton

Quintenna Boone Hampton lived in a little yellow house in a bend of Clark Road, surrounded by her children and her children's children. Nine households of the Hampton clan lived nearby in homes and trailers scattered through the coves of Green Hill, and to all of them she was "Ole Granny."

Other folks knew her affectionately as "Quintenny." When the weather was good, she could be found sitting on her porch quilting, under the apple tree in the front yard enjoying the shade, or in the side yard stringing and snapping beans, surrounded by three large pots, a swarm of little children, and assorted dogs.

Her skin was darkly tanned from years of hard work under the sun in the fields. Although eighty years old, she moved surely, though with a bend in the hip. Her eyes were crackling ginger, full of snap and humor, and occasional thunder when called for.

Her family was her joy. All three boys, who worked in the local mills, settled down nearby, giving her nine grandchildren and eight great-grandchildren, over whom she reigned in country queenly fashion.

The family's claim to pioneer royalty was well founded. Quintenna was a sixth-generation, direct descendant of Daniel Boone. Boone was her maiden name when she met and married Will Hampton. They came to Rutherford County in 1911 from the high mountains of Madison County.

Stringing beans on a hazy, hot July day, she recalled that time. "I come from thirty miles yon side of Asheville in Madison County. Hit's five mile outside Mars Hill—Faust Community. You had to cross Big Ivy and Little Ivy, the yon side of Big Walnut. Law', hit's rough. Back then in a wagon you had to tie a log on the back to stop hit from a-runnin' away with you. Still, I heard one man was kilt when his wagon tore loose."

Quintenna spoke in a pure Western North Carolina mountain brogue that was spiced with Elizabethan phrases and earthy word patterns. Her lilting speech came from a time when talking and story telling were the way people communicated best—and Quintenna used it like an art.

She excused herself by explaining, "Poor folks, they only know how to talk in poor ways." But she spoke with pride of her family. "Ol' Man Garfield Logan always used to tell Will he'd give anything if his children lived near him like our'n did. His sons went hither and yon spread out all over the continent. All our'n settled down right here within hollerin' distance, and hit's might' nice too. I don't reckon hit's been a day that I haven't seen 'em all. Hit's just might' near a little town here now. Hit's pretty well Hamptonville," she laughed, an infectious grin spreading across her face. "Ol' Man Garfield used to say, 'You got the best family I've ever seen—you all live all around together.'

"I always had to go to the fields," she said, "'cause Will, he didn't have help. So I had to let the housework go with a lick and a promise. In those days we absolutely had to work. Why, Will'd cut twenty-one cross ties a day and load 'em in the wagon and then work a half hour in the garden. Cut the cross ties by ax and crosscut saw out of white or red oak—or walnut.

"I started to work when I was six years old. Daddy didn't rush us. He started me out weedin'

the middle of the row. Then when I was seven, I had my own row and my younger sister, Ethel, took *my* middle." She stopped breaking beans to lean back precariously in the green cane-bottom chair. "We used to work at the Cleghorn Woolen Mill in town from six to six. Why, we'd get in the bed and set up talkin' a while to eleven-thirty and then get up at four-thirty in the morning and never think anything about it.

"My young'uns always got up when we did—even if it was four-thirty—and there warn't no fuss. Nowadays they get up at dinnertime. Well, you know hit's like they allus told me. When you've got little children, they're allus trompin' on your toes—then when they're growed up they're trompin' on your heart."

She hoisted a little girl onto her lap and tenderly tied a shoe. "You're nothing but a pet," she teased. "There's a sight of little kids around here, part of 'em down at the river and another part of 'em down at Thompson Pond, fishin' or whatever."

The little great-grandchild in her lap looked up and felt her face. "Ol' Granny, you got too many ugly wrinkles," she said seriously.

Quintenna laughed easily. "Why laws, child, I'm not a-worrin' about wrinkles no more. I'm old I know. But I don't feel a bit old."

But she was old enough to remember talks of Indians, folk medicine, and log-cabin living. "Indians?" said Daniel Boone's great-great-great-great-granddaughter. "Will, he always said he wanted to kill him an Indian 'cause the Indians killed one of his kin-people over in Polk County a long ways back."

About log cabins Quintenna knew only too well. "We lived in a log house right down the holler here a piece. Hit was daubed with mud. That's all they had. And hit was papered with newspapers all around. There was an L built off for the kitchen. But the floor was just planked and

so cracky that when the wind blow'd hit'd pick the quilt that Theodore was sittin' on plumb up off'en the ground.

"The fireplace was all we had to stay warm. But you just didn't stay in there long enough to get cold. Just eat and go out again. And we had plenty of quilts, and always enough to eat. Why you'd just go out and get you a mustard leaf, put a little salt on it, and put that between some cornbread. Laws, it was good.

"Mud was all they had to daub log houses with, and hit worked good. We once't lived in a sawmill shack over on Hampton Road up the Cove Road that had a mud chimney. They'd pile logs around to build it, then pack mud around and let it dry. Then they'd build a big fire in it and them there logs'd burn out, leavin' the mud."

One of Quintenna's skills was her knowledge of natural cures and herb medicines. "Hit used to be we didn't have money to go runnin' off to the doctor. Nowadays they've got to go see a doctor for anything. We didn't have anything to go to a doctor *with*!" Pointing to a lombardy poplar rustling in the front-yard breeze, she instructed, "Yander's a bam-bud tree. Called really the bam-a-Gilead bud tree. Ever since Bud Fowler's little girl got burned up on Hampton Road and he made some bam-bud salve that saved her, I been makin' it for burns. Hit's a-mighty good. Why, you boil the bark down and mix it in with some Vaseline or lard to make a salve." She listed "seven-bark salve" as another burn ointment.

"Sulphur, you buy that at the store and mix hit with molasses and give that to the children, and hit makes a mighty good spring tonic. That's pretty good stuff. Then you can do lots of things with ginseng tea. There used to be some of that growin' down on the wood branch back yonder but hits hard to find now. And sampson snake root is good for the colic in babies. You make a

sweet tea with it by getting the root and dry it out. Then sweeten it with something, and that's good for the asthmy too.

"Wild-cherry-bark tea is a cure for lots of things. Good for the shingles. And golden seal is awful healin' stuff. Yallerroot is good for lots of things like sore throat or sore mouth. But they don't use stuff like that any more. I know as little as anybody in this world, and I've about forgot all I did know," Quintenna laughed.

When it got so hot that stringing beans by the side of the house became unbearable, Quintenna moved to the deep shade of a sagging apple tree in the front yard. She tilted her chair back easily at her favorite angle and reached with one brown arm to steady herself on a low-hanging limb. A collection of barefoot children went giggling by. "You'uns a-fixin' to go off?" she demanded amid a chorus of "good-bye Ol' Granny." At her feet was a plastic toy left in the grass. "When we had kids you'd not see no sech stuff as that, for they were happy with the least little thing. Shucks, Will'd made a wagon out of black-gum limb sawed for wheels and fix that onto a little wagon bed and that'd do 'em fine.

"The first year we lived here we killed eleven rattlesnakes. I remember seein' one crawlin' down the road. 'Will,' I said, 'look yonder at that rattle-snake.' Whoooeey! Hit musta been six feet long. If you ever hear one sing with its rattles, you better watch out. They allus sing when you get near. I'm satisfied that you can take the rattles and put them in a fiddle to make the music better. I know it does, for my daddy had a fiddle with rattlesnake rattles inside," she said.

"I tell you I believe in keeping old things and old ways. Folks seemed like there for a while all they wanted was just new things. Now they want old things again. I never used a store-bought toothbrush in my life. Just git you a little birch sprig and chew on it. Around these parts that's hard to find, so just use black gum—with sody and salt.

"My folks say 'Granny why don't you watch the TV?' but they's just nothin' worth nothin' on TV anymore. I don't care nary a thing about it. I watch the news every mornin' and forgit it every evening."

Quintenna Boone Hampton reflected, "Now that we've got everything a body could want, folks don't seem happy as they used to. Ain't hardly got time to live now-a-days. Have to work all the time, and then they've somewhere's to go after they've quit work. Seems like folks were a whole lot happier back then. Seems like they were.

"I just like to be here—with my people around me—and be able to set in a good shady place and watch so's I can see who's a-goin' by."

G. W. McKee

George William McKee, of Polkville, represented the last of the old school of professional photographers who used glass negatives and blazing flashpowder. He lived by himself in the weather-board homestead where he had worked since 1911. The ninety-one-year-old photographer still kept bees, had his own frame shop where he still turned out a frame now and then, and was still taking pictures. After seventy-two years as a photographer he had his first one-man show in 1972 at a local community college. The exhibit featured his fifty- to seventy-year-old photographs of the area, including family portraits, train wrecks, and passing circuses. It was quite a debut. McKee dressed up in coat and tie for the reception in his honor and proudly greeted folks with his now-antique 6" x 8" view camera.

On the farm, McKee dressed like the farmer he became in the 1930s: overalls, leather cap, and work shirt. Easing down into a straight-back chair in his simple bedroom, which also served as a living room, McKee waved at the browning photographs hung around the room. Taken during the early years of his career, they showed men standing stiffly by the Broad River or in heroic poses atop Chimney Rock—all with that curious statuelike quality typical of old photographs.

"I had to climb up on them rocks," McKee recollected, "with that big ol' camera, and my tripod. I'd have to tell 'em to stand real still. On a sunny day, that might mean five seconds. I'd spread the cloth hood over the back of the camera and look through the ground glass. Then I'd focus that camera and get it good and sharp. Back then we used glass negatives. I'd slip one in there and be ready. We didn't have no light meters back then, so I'd have to guess about the exposures."

His hands cradled an ochre-brown faded photograph lovingly. A young woman in old-fashioned, high-necked garb and with a wistful expression gazed out from behind the glass. "Now, here's my wife. I took this back somewhere's between 1900 and 1920. Photography wasn't that easy back then."

McKee's method for processing his negatives and photographs was as intuitive and unstructured as country biscuit making. "I'd develop 'em in there," he said, wagging his head in the direction of a closet of the old house. "Haven't done any darkroom work in a long time, but that's where I used to do it. Now I used a kerosene lamp with a red glass for my safe light. And I'd take that there glass negative and rock it in the developer with my hands. It'll just start coming up—and get plainer. And when you've got it good," he rocked an imaginary plate in his hands, "then you slip it into the water. And then on to the fix bath so it won't be hurt by the light.

"Of course then when it's dry you gotta make the print. I'd take that negative and put it in this frame and then put the paper in there right against it to make the print." The photograph of his young wife was employed in the lesson.

"They's several ways to make the print. I used the north window to print mine," McKee declared unashamedly. No enlarger costing hundreds of dollars for him. The north window. But McKee's primitive methods worked unfailingly. His negatives were so big and apparently his work was so consistent that sandwiching the

negative and the photographic paper together, making a contact print, proved to be quite adequate. He produced six-inch by eight-inch prints simply by letting window light do the work.

By dead reckoning, interpolation, and sheer experience, he could estimate just the proper time exposure at the window. "After a while, I'd just guess how long it would take—two minutes about—and they all came out just right. But after you do it, it ain't nothin' on paper. You've got to know how to develop it just right.

"I took a whole lotta post cards and what you'd call 'penny pictures' about the size of a postage stamp. But I've stopped my darkroom work now. Send all my pictures to Kodak. And

they've sent me some negatives back not printed out. But I know I could go in that darkroom and do them right. Those fellers up there just don't do it to suit me sometimes."

McKee stopped photographing in the 1930s, when farming became his main livelihood. "Such as it was," he said. He continued to take pictures but not as many as he had earlier. Although he now used an Instamatic, he still had his old equipment. From the darkroom he produced an ancient wooden box containing flash powder—silver nitrate, which was exploded to provide the blinding light that enabled early photographers to take pictures in low-light situations.

"I'd hold some flash powder on a shovel, open

the shutter, and then put a match to this—and it would make you blind with the flash. And he worked," McKee said, bottling the powder up and replacing it on the shelf. "I kept one box just to have, just in case," he winked.

Walking to his frame shop, he squinted in the light of his sunny porch. "F/16," he might have been thinking. But he didn't say. Inside the shop were his angle saw, woodstove, and a life-time of memorabilia collected by a man who delighted in collecting images and faces as well as things.

Taking off his leather cap, he rested by the window. The light outlined his beaklike profile. And he held still. Completely still. As though he were posing for a self-portrait taken with that old wooden-bodied camera, glass negative, cloth bellows, hood, and all.

Ed Norville

W. Ed Norville was the dean of the county's watch and clock repairmen. If he couldn't fix a clock or a watch, then, as Ed would say, "Hit's plumb busted."

His tiny shop sat by his house. Inside drawers and cigar boxes were stacked to the ceiling. On the walls several sets of deer antlers served as racks for rifles and fishing equipment. Much of the floor space was taken up by a woodstove and a thirties-vintage radio.

"You feelin' happy this morning?" Ed asked,

as he hunched over his work desk, examining the insides of a watch. "Yeah, I'm feelin' a little bit alive, myself." The shop was darkened except for the light of two half-drawn windows and the makeshift lamp that illuminated the work space. Strewn in ordered chaos across the desk were every sort of tweezers, pliers, picks, tiny wrenches, and unnamable tools.

"We three boys all had a talent to fix things," he began. "If you ain't got a talent you better not start up at something. I been a-doin' this as a

hobby-like for fifty-six years. I started with an old cheap watch. Tore it down fifteen or twenty times 'til I knew how it ticked.

"I'm eighty-four-past, and I can still take the little lady watch apart. These here is my wife's glasses. I use 'em for bifocals. Don't need 'em 'cept to do fine work. I can read good without glasses. My eyesight's just comin' back. Guess I'm like my grandmother. She could still thread the smallest needle at a hundred and one. She lived to be a hundred and five, six months, and eight days." Returning to the subject of eyesight, he said, "But lookin' at metal pieces and readin' print is two different things."

Ed's face was crinkled and furrowed like an eroded cornfield. A couple of day's growth of white stubble sprouted on his chin. He stopped his work, leaned back on the piano stool, and turned grey-green eyes to the window. His face took on a masklike, timeless expression, as though he were looking back at something only he could see. "Lived all my life, 'cept for five years, right here in Rutherford County. Five years I was in Dysartsville. The winter of 1917–18. Man, it was cold, Great God. It went down to eighteen below zero. I got up at four A.M. to go feed the mules 'cause I knew they'd need the food to keep them warm. They had ice frozen on their

mustaches as big as that pencil," he said, pulling a lead pencil from a drawer.

"It was the same year I built this here desk." He ran his hands over the aged dark wood of the watch repair desk with its many intricate drawers and white porcelain knobs. "Hit's even got an apron drawer I can pull out so's to catch things I might drop. The cloth catches it instead of the floor.

"There, I did get it back together," he said with satisfaction, securing the back of the watch to its case. "You know it's delicate work here in a watch. You can't go to punching and gouging on them things without you'll do something bad.

"Back then was tough times for poor folks. Money was scarce. If young folks had to go through what I did when I was a boy, they'd be something happenin' more. The young generation don't know nothin' about what our forefathers went through."

Shunning retirement, the craftsman said, "If you're brought up in labor from childhood on up and then you quit circulatin', why then, you'll go right down."

His nimble fingers paced through the tools strewn on the red linoleum work space. Finding the proper instrument, he opened the back of a century-old wall clock. "Oh, my gawd. Would you just look at this. What I call bum work. Some repairmen do terrible things," he said, pointing to the shoddy soldering job somebody had done.

"Well," he pondered, like a doctor passing a life-or-death prognosis over a patient in intensive care, "it's gonna be a little agg'avatin' to fix, but," he scratched a hoary chin and squinted at the patient's insides, "but I believe I can do it."

Taking the works out of the case, he tentatively fingered the brass gears. "If you don't understand a thing, don't monkey with it. A clock's a fine thing. Gotta know whatcher doin'.

I'll have to take some fine metal I have and make a new post here, saw it just so with this hacksaw, and then get it to runnin' so's the pendulum will be plumb."

He bent over the bright face of the clock, the bench and work area splashed with light from a homemade ceiling lamp. It hung right down practically in his face. He grinned for the first time. "Remember I used to have a paper lamp shade. And once't I had to use this yere alchy-hol lamp to heat up to set some jewels. The paper shade caught on fire, and I had to wiggle around a little. So I built me this one out of a piece of old tin dishpan, I reckon.

"I farmed a little every year. Keep up seven head of cattle now. Still do some dairy work. Do that myself." He also did some carpentry over

the years. "I helped build many of the buildings in Westminster. Helped build the gym and school-house here at Sunshine. Sawed the end of my thumb off one time. It didn't feel good, but it was done so quick. If it had been done by degrees, it'd a-been rough," he smiled.

Ed turned back to his work as the cuckoo clock on the wall blurted out the hour. The rain plinked on the tin roof as a trio of clocks played a rhythmic cadence with the raindrops. He picked up one of the bell jars that covered a mysterious looking set of tools. "These are staking tools," he said. "I can't tell you all the things you can fix with that piece of plunder. But I guess it's like my brother used to say. . . . I just like to piddle around sometimes."

Hoyle Greene

When the air tingled with the first hints of autumn and little green apples got about the size of hen's eggs, Hoyle Greene made his cider. And not just any cider either. This concoction of Greene's was the essence of the magic fall season—tangy and sour, it conjured up drowsy warm childhood autumn days.

It was Greene's own childhood experience of helping his folks make cider each fall that prompted him to start making his own cider several years ago. "I just studied it out," the seventy-seven-year-old merry figure chirped. "Got this here old Blackhawk corn shucker at the bone-yard. Then I scalded it to get the spiders and sech out."

Greene began his ritual on this late summer day ("Fall came two weeks early this year.") by putting a homemade sign out beside the front door of his home in Forest City which instructed visitors, "I am around back working."

Latching the front screen door, he winked conspiratorially. "Now, we've put up the all-clear sign, here we go." Hefting two buckets full of

plump but not-too-big green apples, he made his way through the kitchen and out to the back porch, then down the steep back-porch stairs, "Careful, there, you'll peel your back," he cautioned. "I know, I've done it."

Greene's backyard looked like he had a cleaning woman who came daily to tidy up. An apple tree shaded a neatly swept sandy plot, a favorite work space. A woodshed made from an old discarded bedstead and a sawmill Greene built just big enough to saw wood for his woodstove sat to the side. A neat garden with a carefully dug irrigation ditch bordered the yard.

"Been a bachelor all my days," Greene announced. "Old enough now to sleep by myself," he added with a gleeful smile. "I've had to learn how to fend for myself.

"Under the shade of the ol' apple tree . . ." he mused to himself, as he began puttering back and forth, assembling the first stages of his cider press. "Now, here's the elbow grease." He brought out a sturdy stool and mounted the cast-iron apple grinder firmly in place. "Nobody'd

ever thought of using a corn-sheller for this until me, I reckon," he said, placing a bucket of apples on a nearby chair. "Can't use big'uns. Gotta have apples 'bout the size of hen's eggs." Popping the first apple into the machine, he turned the crank with his right hand and shoved the apple into the grinding teeth with an oak stick. The apple going through Greene's machine sounded like a horse chewing a hand-fed apple: a delicious chomping sound—full of small, juicy explosions.

In his worn but starched, clean Pointer overalls, he squinted through his tiny spectacles as he cranked away and churned the apples. It was a hypnotic scene: apple juice spraying like water from a slightly leaky garden hose and Greene narrating the operation.

"This here's the right size—some of 'em are too big. Shove 'em in like this. Them teeth grab right a-holt. Sometimes the juice flies and gets on my headlights," he smiled through his wire-rims. "Somebody wanted me to get an electric motor to turn this handle, but I told them that's the way to get your hand ground off. Besides, if'n I used electricity, I'd have to pay for it. This is pure elbow grease—one manpower.

"These apples came in two weeks earlier this year than they ordinar'ly do. Yeah—we're gettin' going here." He dropped the apples into the grinder one by one. "On this day, the twenty-third of August, nineteen hunnerd and seventy three. Peacetime. . . . Well, not peacetime, it's worktime," he quipped, enjoying himself.

"I been livin' here for seven year. I see'd how these was good apple trees, so I trim'd 'em back to make 'em bigger and better, and they had more of 'em. It did. Kept cuttin' back the honey-suckle, and it's been a-havin' good apples ever since."

By this time, a sizable porridge of crushed apple pulp lay in the pan underneath the grinder. Greene popped the last apple and announced,

"Now then, now then . . . right over here, right over here . . . I got this stool I made, and I'll mount this press on it. Where's my hammer? And here's my screwdriver." He moved to the second part of the operation, the pressing of the pulped apples. "Now, said the blind man . . . said the blind man, coming up."

He poured the pulp into the handmade press box and set it beneath the press. "Had a feller thread this here pipe, and I worked this crank myself," he said, placing a thick slab of pine board between the press and the apple pulp. "More elbow grease. Now then, we go to town. Now . . . and there . . . she . . . comes. . . ." The words came out between turns of the crank, and soon the sweet dark juice ran in rivulets out from under the press, onto a warped pine board with a hand-carved trough, and down into a pan.

"Just like pressing a bale of cotton. Like to know how much pressure I've got there. That's good ol' cider, sure is. There it comes—sour apple cider. They used to have a song way back yonder, 'Jefferson Davis, hung him on a sour apple tree,' but I don't know what it was that he done wrong."

Greene removed the panful of juice and carried it to the top of the nearby power-saw table, where he strained it. "Use a regular old-fashioned milk strainer. Gotta put my finger in there. Don't like to, but it gets so thick here." He stirred the collected mashings to permit the juice to stream into a quart mason jar. "That there's vitamin A, if you wanta call it that way."

He held up the full quart jar of dark, sweet-smelling liquid, rared back and squinted at the cider authoritatively then summed up the whole operation, "Apple cider. Made in the shade—stirred with a lemonade spade."

Hoyle Greene maintained that since he was raised in Danieltown, he had never "lost that

39

country wiggle." For him, "It just wouldn't be right for it to be gettin' on to fall without me makin' a run or two." And taking an old battered tin cup, he sampled the afternoon's labor, smacked his lips, and concluded, "Hit'll shore make you bite your tongue."

Snuffy Jenkins

Snuffy Jenkins came home every second Sunday to cut hair—and to visit. At sixty-seven, Snuffy was widely recognized as one of the pioneers of bluegrass. Driving a pickup over the rough dirt road that led to Snuffy's home, former deputy sheriff and bluegrass music devotee Ben Humphries talked about the music. "It's pure music—natural music. People express themselves with it. It tells the story of everyday people's lives. If you listen to those old songs, you can get their troubles, trials, joys and sorrows, and happiness. You get it all.

"I just think of some old boy who is working for his dad and plows when he says plow—all day long, dawn 'til dark. Then he comes in that evening, bone tired, feeds his mule, and gets himself something to eat. Then he might go down to the branch and take off his brogans and wash off his durned feet.

"Then he'd go up on the porch and play a banjo or guitar. And that's what it's all about. That's what bluegrass means to me. It's everybody's music. It's just plain talk put to music.

"Now Snuffy," he continued, shouting over the rattle of the truck on the washboard road, "comes from a musical family. The whole family's an old-time string band that won't quit. Snuffy literally came off the Broad River playing the banjo like nobody ever heard before. He was picking the three-fingered banjo like this before Scruggs was even born. Snuffy's sort of the granddaddy of the banjo pickers as far as I'm concerned."

Ben's pickup made the last bend in the road and careened into a dirt driveway, which opened into a broad, sandy yard. An immense white oak shaded the Jenkins family homeplace, birthplace of bluegrass's lesser-known cousin, Broad River music.

"That's what they oughta call it," Ben said doggedly. "Broad River music. It didn't come from Kentucky. That three-finger picking style Scruggs made popular was invented right here in Cleveland and Rutherford counties, and Snuffy Jenkins was one of the first pickers to go at the banjo like that—way before Scruggs did."

The Jenkinses were waiting on the front porch for Ben's arrival. After the howdies and handshakes, Snuffy pulled from a battered old case his most prized possession, a venerable Gibson Mastertone five-string banjo, which he bought for forty dollars in the thirties.

"Been offered two thousand dollars for it," he recited proudly. "I'll just pick and grin some," he wisecracked, settling himself into an iron chair in the front yard. The five strings chimed in on "Lonesome Road Blues" and then "Cripple Creek." *Chimed* is the right word—Snuffy's banjo was ringing like a church carillon.

The kids tumbled out of the house to hear the music on the porch. Snuffy's brother Orin joined in with a guitar, and the banjo was passed around, while the old granddad, Roy Jenkins, shuffled in and out of the house with armloads of wood.

After they ran through some old tunes, Snuffy paused and began to talk about how he got started in the thirties with the Crazy Water Crystal's Barn Dance Show on WSOC in Charlotte. He had gone to Harris High School and learned his picking from the two men who really originated the three-finger picking style. Moving to

Columbia, South Carolina, he gained minor fame on a radio program and made a couple of albums. "But I quit that on account of my health. . . . I was starving to death," he said wryly, drawing an easy laugh from his audience.

After a couple more rounds of banjo passing, eighty-three-year-old Roy Jenkins came out on the porch, and everyone begged him to play the fiddle. Roy, according to a favorite family tale, started the Jenkins family musical tradition by walking all the way from Harris to Forest City to buy his first fiddle. He couldn't play a note

when he bought it, but by the time he had walked all the way home along the railroad tracks, he could play respectably.

Protesting vigorously—while Orin rosined up the bow—that he couldn't play anymore, Roy winked, grabbed the fiddle, and led off an old tune. "There's no fiddler like an old fiddler," said somebody on the porch, as Roy sawed into "Cripple Creek," joined by Snuffy on banjo and Orin on guitar.

The whole porch was bouncing when Roy decided it was time to see if he could still buck-dance. Handing his fiddle to Ben Humphries,

the patriarch of the Jenkins clan got up and clogged in the sandy front yard. The front door slammed and Roy's wife came out in her apron, unabashedly stomping her heels in shuffle-stomp time, while everyone clapped and laughed.

The tune over and the dance gone, Grandpa Jenkins flopped down in a chair, panting amid cheers and back slapping. "Grandpa, why are you huffing?" one of the children inquired.

"Boy," Roy Jenkins eye-balled the youngster in mock ferocity, "you shake these durn brogans around for a while and you'll know why!"

Carl Lawing

Carl Lawing had owned Gilkey's Mill since 1926. Hard times closed the place down in 1935. But constant to the end, Carl Lawing, eighty-two this September, had visited the mill every day for over forty years.

The mill stood four stories high in a thick beech and maple forest. Tufts of green moss highlighted the weathered wood. Blackened windows with glass all gone faced the dirt road. It was built some time in the 1800s by a Dr. Gilkey even before Gilkey was Gilkey. "Used to be called Millwood then," Lawing said confidently. "They named it after the doctor when the post office came and they found there was already another Millwood somewhere in North Carolina."

The mill apparently fell into disrepair for a period. It was rebuilt, Lawing remembered, in the spring of 1909. The Gilkey's Mill then was named after its new builder, Jim Geer. Later Geer went into business with two other men, and the mill was called the Geer, Dixon, and Tanner Mill.

Carl Lawing lived just down the narrow dirt road, within easy walking distance of the mill. "When I was fifteen, this is where all the boys hung out. There wasn't no other place to go. It was old times, I'm sayin' *old* times. I just holpt Jim Geer until I learnt the whole operation."

The mill's history closely paralleled the history of the Rutherfordton-Marion highway that runs nearby. Before the turn of the century the main road passed just outside the mill's front door. It was only a wagon path, fording the creek in several places as it went north. "This was the old Jamestown road, it was called," Lawing recalled, "but they changed it twice, away from here and t'other side of the creek."

Lawing bought the mill in 1926, but bad luck prevailed against him and his mill, as the economy and the location of the road proved very unpre-dictable. In 1928 they moved the road even farther north, and in 1929 the bottom of the economy dropped out. "I hung on to '35, and then closed her down," he said.

But what a sight and sound it must have been when the mill was running. Something of the magic of the mill remained in the special look Carl had when he unlocked the heavy angle and nailed front doors for his daily visit.

Inside it was a tantalizing museum of cob-webby and time-dusted machinery, chains, leather conveyor belts, wooden chutes, levers, troughs, and wheels—all silent, still, and just waiting for the rush of the creekwater down the race from the mill's dam—long storm blasted and reduced to so many creek rocks.

The afternoon sun squinted through the gold-frosted windows to show the way that Carl Lawing knew only too well. "Used to have to carry kerosene lanterns around with us. The rest of the time we just used winder light."

He visited each machine in turn—flour bins, cleaners, smutters, cob-breakers, sifters, sorters, and always a forest of wooden chutes jutting through the ceiling from one level to another. Lawing talked knowingly about the mill's running with the precision of a backwoods engineer.

He seemed to be hearing the clatter of the corn through the chutes, the shushing of the wheat ris-ing and falling through the wooden avenues, the gnashing of rocky teeth, and always the rush of the water and the energizing roar of the turbine wheel in the basement.

Now there was only the creek. All else was silent, save the water, still flowing just as power-fully as it had flowed seventy years before when the place was blond and spanking new with fragrant, fresh-sawed heart pine.

Maybe that's the way Carl saw his mill. Not decaying and sagging and piled with unused rust-

ing machines, but vibrant and thronging with life and activity and productivity. "Folks used to come from all over—from Westminster and Centennial Road with their wheat and corn. Came on wagon, horseback, and walkin' foot. Them was old days."

Clayton Norville

Clayton Norville, of Westminster, walked slowly but purposefully from Long's Store across the highway and into the big machine shop that hulked under three large oaks. "I suppose it's an awful mess in here," he remarked. "Things just pile up. . . . I shoulda cleaned up." He reloaded with Favorite chewing tobacco. Then, stuffing the red pouch in a back pocket, he went to work.

It was common knowledge among the locals that Norville could build anything he put his mind to. That included a planer, a tractor, a cane stripper, a router, a thread grinder, and parts for his cotton gin. He carved the gears out of white pine or poplar and then sent them all off to a foundry to have the parts cast in steel and when he put it all together, it worked. He ran his shop on one of the county's first gasoline engines in 1905, long before power and lights came to Rutherford, much less to Westminster.

Norville worked his way through Brittain Academy by working part time in a machine shop. He learned his physics and machinery there at the school. He worked for a time building bridges for the state. In 1918 he designed and built a cotton gin; in his time he also was a surveyor. Then after the Second World War he and his sons went into the concrete block business.

At eighty-six he still pursued his love of machines, tools, and blacksmithing. He did a bit of surveying now and then, and today he was repairing an old muzzle-loading rifle that had not been fired in longer than he could remember.

"I ought to go up to the house and sit in a rocking chair. I'm not feeling as good as I used to. Guess I ought to go to the hospital, but I don't like to go," he said, half to himself, stopping to stare out a cobwebbed window. His shop was unique: all dark and dusty with lathes and metalworking machines standing in the gloom. In one lighted corner Norville bent over a tool-cluttered workbench, his anvil and furnace nearby.

Light fell through two large dusty windows and a bare lightbulb outlined his bent figure. He wore faded overalls, grey work shirt, and a black felt slouch hat. The eyes that peered out from the large wire-rim glasses were not the eyes of an old man; they caught the glint of the light bulb, and somehow one got the feeling that here masqueraded a boy who never outgrew his love for tinkering. His hands were hands that had spent a lifetime of doing. Norville used them constantly and precisely.

He had spent most of Thursday working on the bullet mold, getting it just right, and had made a couple of balls to fit the old gun. Friday he had worked all morning finishing the rifle, which was given to him by his father. He pointed to the top of the rifle, where the signature of its maker was etched, "Philip H. Groce." Its long, octagonal barrel proved its age. "It's well over one hundred years old," Norville said, pulling back the firing pin. "Here it takes a percussion cap. We'll shoot it when I get done. I'd like to fahr it today," he said, gently tightening the rifle in the vise.

He bent silently to his work. Inside the high-ceilinged shop, the only sound was the rain dripping off the oaks onto the tin roof. He drilled a hole in the side of the gun, talking to himself, "Now, that ain't gonna do. Gotta find a little nail." He puttered around the shop slowly but surely, finding bits and hammers just where he had left them that morning or years before.

The place was once a modern machine shop. Now time had taken over, and only in that one corner did the spark keep going. "Piddlin'" was what he called it. "Gotta have good light," he muttered. "Can't see now as good as I used to. Gotta wear glasses. . . . There, that's done."

He picked up the rifle, turning it expertly in his boney hands.

To measure out the right amount of powder to load the gun, he used an old .38 shell. First he pried off the slug. Then he prepared to get the cap out by setting it off. Turning from his workbench to his blacksmith furnace, he gathered up some bits of paper and placed them in the ash pit. He poured in a shot of kerosene, lighted it, and started up the bellows. Immediately a tongue of flame shot up the tin chimney and smoke billowed out from the chimney lip and puffed about the shop, its acrid smell adding to the flavor of the place.

Norville let the fire subside before he examined the cap in the coals; then he wound the electric bellows back up and the fire shot high again. "Back when I was a boy they had leather bellows, and you'd have to pump the lever up and down. The first shop I had I put some Sears

and Roebuck leather bellows on my furnace. Later on, I got this electric motor hitched up— heated a lot of iron," he said.

While Norville was talking, the cap suddenly exploded, popping across the room onto the sod floor. The fire went out, and he took the shell outside to let it cool. Then loading it with black firing powder, he poured a measure down the long rifle barrel. Next he carefully cut a cloth swab and wrapped the round ball in it; he stuffed the wad down the gun with a wooden ramrod. Finally, he pulled back the firing pin, examined the firing area, and placed a cap on the mount.

Norville propped the old rifle against a saw-horse and walked about twenty-five yards to another barn, where he made a target and taped it to a two-by-four. Then he walked back to his sitting place, raised the gun to a propping post, and aimed it across the yard.

The gun cracked, amid much smoking and

sparking. "Fired too soon," he muttered. "Knew I was off. Can't see like I used to." The old man, who "can't see like he used to," missed a one-inch diameter target at twenty-five yards by one inch. He called that a miss.

"That's the first time the gun's been fired in a long time," he said, satisfied. He looked down at the gun where neighboring gunsmith Philip Groce had carefully carved his name a century before. "People used to make everything themselves. By hand. People were accountable for what they made. A boy would sign on with a gunsmith or a cabinetmaker, and he'd stay with it until he learned his trade. Now, you don't know who makes what. Nobody's responsible for what they do."

He sat down on a sawhorse and leaned on the long rifle. "I can't walk too far, and I can't work too hard. I used to do a sight of surveying, but I've got now where I give out walking over the hills. But I can still piddle around here in the shop a-making things for people."

Norville shoved his hat back on his head and watched the traffic whiz by on Highway 64. "The country used to depend on blacksmiths once," he said slowly. "There was mules to be shod, maddoxes to be sharpened, wheels to be made. They were essential at one time. Country couldn't get along without the blacksmith."

He stood up slowly and, turning his back on the modern age, walked back into his shop, where things were still made by hand and a man was at home with his work.

Horace Vickers

Horace Vickers, sitting proudly in his '24 T-Model Ford, pulled out his pouch of Stud, tapped it with his right forefinger to prod the tobacco out onto the paper, and deftly rolled a cigarette with one hand. Putting the string of the pouch to his mouth, he yanked the tobacco bag shut with a grimace.

"Ain't never had another car," the seventy-nine-year-old Vickers said, reaching into his faded jean jacket pocket for a kitchen match. "This here has been the family car since 1924." He scratched the match on the rusty steel of the T-Model's steering wheel and lighted half of the cigarette. "Yup, I got her from Asbury Motor Corporation in '24. Swapped in my '23—it was a cranker, this new 'un had a starter—so I gave 'em the '23 and one hundred dollars. It's out of shape now, but it's gone many a mile. Both of us is ailin' a bit," Vickers said, reaching for his second match.

Vickers's son Britt put one foot on the running board and drawled proudly, "Yup, he raised us six young'uns on that T-Model and a hammer." Vickers, a carpenter by trade, used the car to haul lumber. Its dented fenders told of many loads of wood. "I've hauled enough lumber to build any ten-room house," he said.

The remarkable thing about the car was that it wasn't restored or rejuvenated. It was the same car he had bought tags for every year and driven about just like anybody else on the road. "It ain't been a month since he drove it," Britt said. And he added, "You've heard you could keep a T-model running with just a piece of baling wire and a pair of pliers? Well, since they've gone to baling hay with twine, it's pretty hard."

The car was, or had been, black. Now, it was a dusty ochre. No shine, no fancy chrome work—just good old car. The right fender of Vickers's car was torn up a bit. "That's where I

ran into a ditch. Dog got in my way. Must have been waving my cane at that dog. Ran off the road. Broke the axle. Had to get a new one. That baling wire's under there to hold them hickeys." He pointed with his cane to the one-spring suspension, aided by the twisted wire.

The radiator had some curious white objects cemented in its grill here and there. "That's cottonseed. Plugs up leaks. And I guess that's a load of Stud in there. That stops leaks as good as anything I know."

The old two-part windshield carried two inspection stickers. One was for 1948, the other was for the current year. Britt recounted that when they took the T-Model in for its inspection, the man said, "I don't know a durn thing about this car. I'm gonna have to put a sticker on it."

Britt cranked up the four coils, which began humming. "That's the coils a-singin'," Vickers explained. "Here comes one of the pit crew," Britt said, as Leroy Earley walked up the drive. Britt's son-in-law Leroy helped keep the car running.

It required a good push to get the car rolling down the rutted drive. With Britt driving, the T-Model coughed and sputtered in protest. At the last possible moment, the motor caught. "Hear those rods?" Britt said. Whoever sat in "shotgun" had to keep the little door shut by hanging his right leg over the side of the car. Britt manipulated the spark and gas levers, pushed the far-left pedal all the way down for first gear, and released the hand brake. The car tottered off down the road like an old pensioner on his daily constitutional.

Britt let the pedal out altogether, and it jumped into drive, clattered up a slow climb, and conked out. "Puzzonk!" went the horn as Britt signaled for help. "Let's look and see if we're out of gas. You'll have to get up. Don't you know where

the gas tank is?" he asked, grinning. He pulled up the seat, and there was the tank under the wooden floor boards.

Leroy arrived with the pick-up truck, hitched up a chain, and pulled the T-Model to the top of the hill. On the roll downhill, the car leapt to life again, so Britt unhitched, and the ancient Ford roared home, fidgeting and bouncing down the hill. He turned in at the house, and the T-Model charged up the drive to the waiting garage.

Britt turned the car off. In the silence of the garage the T-Model seemed instantly asleep again. Unless you had seen it, you would never have known that it had just been out romping on the roads.

Vickers sat on his front porch and waved his red flyswatter in good-bye. "Well, now you can tell 'em you rode in a T-Model," he called from his rocker.

The Millard Family

"Gettup thar, Kate!" the blue-bonneted woman urged gruffly. Resuming its plodding pace, the mule pulled the lead pole in a wide arc around the cane mill, where Mattie Millard fed fresh-cut sugarcane into the grinding gears and Rebecca Millard pitchforked the pulp from the other end. Mountains of crushed cane were piled head high on every side of the mule-driven mill, the last of its kind in Rutherford County. Joe Millard, a stolid sixty-five-year-old farmer who prided himself in this operation, had been making molasses this way since "the early part of the thirties."

On this cold October morning the molasses making was in full gear. Each of the four Millard sisters took a part. Ida brought armloads of cane to the mill, while Mattie fed it in. Becky forked the remains out, and Etta collected the sweet cane juice in metal buckets, which she carried down the hill to the furnace for cooking.

There she poured the juice through a burlap bag strainer stretched over a wooden bucket, which was punctured to let the juice trickle out into one end of the pan. Heated by a wood-fired furnace, the cane juice began to steam and boil, sending up a sweet, pungent cloud of white smoke. Etta scraped off the green skimmings and slopped them in a hole, while Joe tended the far end of the boiling pan, where the cane juice was already beginning to thicken into molasses.

There had been a light freeze the night before, and the morning was windy. It swept the cane vapors away from the boiling pan like ragged ghosts. Etta's and Joe's glasses fogged up. "Can't make 'lasses with glasses on," said Joe, as he pocketed his.

Absorbed in their work, they talked little. Mattie sang a little tune to herself as she fed the cane into the mill, but the only other sounds were the wind in the high oaks and the rhythmic clinking of the mule harness chain.

Joe interrupted his silence to talk of weather and molasses making. "I dread a stout wind," he said. "Remember the second Sunday in October twen'y years ago. It plumb froze. And the wind was bad. Hit's mighty disagreeable.·. . . No, it's not too cold today. Warm here by the furnace. I never know'd a man to freeze to death making molasses." Occasionally, he stoked the long rock furnace with more split pine slabs, and the resulting fire sent the cane juice into furious boilings.

"Everybody used to have their own cane patch." Men traveled the county with portable mills to make each farmer's molasses. Joe named some of the old-time molasses makers—Bill Jack Beheler and Ol' Man Scoggins.

Millard liked to work by the moon. "By my experience, I find that the best 'lasses are made when the full moon is on the decrease. If they're made on the new of the moon, they'll go to sugar, and they'll go to foam if you make them at the full of the moon."

Molasses could be used for many things but one of Joe's favorites was molasses sweet bread. His sisters had their own recipe. "To make it, you have to have strong 'lasses. Not what I'd call good 'lasses. Hit's gotta be strong to give the bread the right sort of whang," Joe said.

By early afternoon, the mule was sweating, Joe had shed his overcoat, and the cane juice in

the far end of the " 'lassy pan" was bubbling in sweetness. "Hit won't be long now," Joe said, holding up his skimming paddle. From the end dripped the lazy golden globules of the first molasses, thick and rich. Joe uncorked the end of the pan, and the brown liquid flowed out into a five-gallon lard bucket, strained again through a cloth sieve.

"Cold juice coming in one end and 'lasses out the other," Joe said simply. It took sixteen gallons of raw cane juice to make one gallon of molasses. It also took a cord of wood to make a batch and two mules working shifts on the cane mill.

The fruit of their labor was delicious. Joe dipped a freshly cut piece of cane in the still-warm molasses and beamed at the first taste. "Hit'll take the hair off'n your tongue."

Littleberry Hines

Except for the pounding truck traffic, the world rolled by a little slower at Hines's Service Station on the banks of the Broad River. With his faithful, crusty-eyed dog George, Littleberry Hines, who recently turned eighty was content to sit in the doorway with a good bowl-full of Prince Albert and smoke pensively on his rutted pipe.

Hines's place was an eddy just out of the swirl created by two streams crossing—one, the muddy Broad, and the other, the churning highway. Hines, a leaf caught in the peaceful eddy, took it easy and liked it that way.

"Shoot, I don't mind telling you my age. . . . If'n I did I would have told you it was none of your business," he laughed. "I built this place in 1956 to give me something to do and so's I could see people. I worked all my life farming and sawmilling. I reckon if I'd have gone and sat down in the house after sawmilling when I got to retirement age, I'd have been dead or crazy by now. It's just an idea of mine, but some people should go on working."

Hines, who insisted that friends leave off the "mister" when talking to him, loaded his pipe carefully behind the counter and lighted the bowl after several tries with wooden matches, then went to sit in one of the sagging cane chairs.

George came and rested his muzzle in Hines's lap, staring up at his master and slapping his tail against the drink cooler in a contented cadence. "All's I know is he's just dog," Hines said. George closed his eyes and sighed as if he knew he was being talked about. "He's a good dog. Oh, he does what I tell him, but you better not come in here scuffling about . . ." Just then a truck backfired out on the highway. That sent George out the door yowling at the possible intruder, all eyes and teeth and very important. He came back quite satisfied with himself and plopped down in the doorway.

Inside the store, the tools of the trade adorned the walls and festooned the windows—fan belts, brake washers in dusty jars, Goody headache powder signs, old Pepsi Generation posters, and an ancient wooden and glass candy chest. Out front a massive hickory nut tree was turning into gold.

A red Mustang pulled in and donged the service station bell. Hines walked out slowly and performed his duties, cranking and punching the gas pump to life and nozzling the hose into the tank for four dollars worth of high test. Then he came back in and sat down, keeping his gray, felt slouch hat pulled down over the face. He wore green work shirt and pants, with a pair of broad, old-fashioned, light-green suspenders.

Next a Comet sedan pulled in. Spencer, a crony of Hines's, sauntered into the store and beckoned, "You still living?"

Hines grinned, "Yeah, how 'bout you?"

Their conversation was that of friends, idle speculation about the weather and informal checking on each other.

"Whole lot of frost down here?" his friend asked.

"Some. . . . It comes sooner down along the river bottoms."

"Had any rain?"

"Not a big sight."

The sun broke through the clouds. Spencer and Hines gazed out the window. The traffic continued shushing by. Trucks roared by, in a

hurry to get up the hill to the South Carolina line a mile to the south.

"Well I guess I'll be nosing off," Spencer said. "Looks like it'll be clearing off back up in the mountains."

Hines nodded his goodbye and went to write up the credit gas sale in a dusty card file. "Don't rush off," he added, half to himself, half to Spencer, already out of earshot.

Will McKissick

Will McKissick, who said he thought he was about sixty-nine, had been a journeyman spike driver on the railroads for over forty years. "It's been forty-four years, leastwise as I can count," he said. He was the senior member of a gang that followed the roads up and down the east side of the Appalachians, taking work where they found it.

Huge modern equipment did most railroad maintenance. Run by one man, they sent up cyclones of dust and grit. Steel drivers, rail lifters, tie grabbers—all in one machine. Modern technology had come to the railroad. But some jobs were too small to make moving in all that big equipment profitable, so gangs like the one Will traveled with were called in.

Putting down ties one day at the main crossing in Spindale, the crew followed an order that bordered on ritual. Will, by seniority, put down the first spike on the newly laid tie. Hefting the heavy hammer gracefully, he quickly positioned the spike. Then he and another man traded strokes to sink it deep into the wood.

Will's old-fashioned blunt hammer made a flat "whank" sound, while the slim-headed hammer of his partner made a "kwing" sound. "Whank-kwing, whank-kwing," they increased their tempo and drove the spike home in twelve blows. Will never missed—he never misses. "Just makes for more work," he said.

"Swing it again. She ain't down yet. Go on," Will directed his partner, one-fourth his age.

"Shoot, that's already down, Will," the younger man teased.

66

"Shhhh, what do you know," he retorted, as the crew broke into laughter. "I been a steel-drivin' man since before you were even born."

Will's bearing was one of command. He might not have been the foreman, or even a gang boss. But he was, nevertheless, in charge, just by virtue of his years. His natural dignity carried an authority beyond that of official titles. One youth even called him "Mr. McKissick." But it was a first-name basis sort of job. Their railroad talk was thick with raw-edged expletives—a working man's lingo.

"Oh yeah, I been workin' for a long time with a bunch of *boys*," he emphasized the last word disparagingly. "In my time I seen 'em come 'n' go. Been pall bearer to a bunch of 'em. They done gone over yonder."

Their good-natured banter carried them through the workday, while in the background the railroad crossing warning alarm rang incessantly. In the midday heat, Will paused several times, once leaning his weight on his hammer and another time placing one foot, housed in a leather shoe, on the ground and propping the other foot, clad in a different kind of shoe, up on the rail. From his back pocket he produced a once-yellow bandana and mopped his broad face. Then spitting on his palms and rubbing them together like a pitcher rubbing the rosin bag, he grasped the shaft again and swung his hammer back into action.

Robertson Bailey

"Hershel Bailey came around the other day, watching me make chairs and allowed as how he'd like to learn. But I told him, 'If you learn how to be a chairmaker, you'll be a little bit more Bailey.'" Robertson Bailey put down his aged broad hatchet and chuckled about that. "Yessir, a little bit more Bailey.

"Y'see, all us Baileys used to be chairmakers. It was a family trade you might say. I learned it from my father and my grandfather. If our family made a chair, I can look at it and might near tell it's one of ours."

Bailey of Rock Springs Community had begun making chairs by hand again. "I'm outa practice," he apologized, deftly fitting a rocker into pegs. "I been quit for twenty years. Yes, I can tell if it's a Bailey chair—by the way the nubs is cut. Oh, they's a lotta things you gotta know from start to finish. But it's coming back. See, part of the problem is the tools. You've got to have special tools like they don't even make anymore to make chairs right. So I been looking around. Collecting—and making my own."

His workshop was an open-sided shed with semicircular arrangement of draw horse, work bench, piles of white-oak splits, a sharpening stone, and six newly finished white-oak rockers, all completely handmade, from the turns down to the white-oak seat "twill" to the whimsically carved rockers.

Outside on the ground was a fire bed, a chopping block, an ax with a homemade handle, and a curious gangly contraption of saplings and ropes. "That's my turn lathe," Bailey said proudly. "Had to build it from memory." He stepped

up to the machine, fixed a chair turn in place, and began to pump the bottom board with his right foot. A rope attached to a limber sapling overhead wound around the turn, and Bailey's foot pumping spun the piece of wood so that he could cut—probably the world's oldest lathe design.

He whacked the chair's posts or main four pieces out of seasoned white oak with an ax and maul. The maul pounded the ax through the white oak, which split true and straight. "It's got to be thoroughly dry," Bailey instructed between blows of the maul. "If your rounds and posts aren't dry, your chair won't be no 'count at all."

Getting good wood turned out to be an unexpected problem. "We don't have the kind of timber we used to have thirty-five years ago," he said. "I look for little oaks that grew slow and have a small grain that will split easily for seat bottoms. But now the little oaks grow so fast that the grain's too large. I never thought about it until I went back to chairin', and now I see ain't nobody in this country got any timber to speak of anymore."

Turning to the draw horse, another creation of Bailey's, he showed how to carve the chair backs. The draw horse held the ladder back in place with a big set of clamps, which resembled a giant nutcracker controlled by the feet. Then when the back pieces were ready, Bailey bent them by heating them over the fire. "They bend just as easy as you please then.

"If you'd been around back in the thirties," he said, "you woulda seen lots of fellas doing this. It was a good sideline back then when we couldn't get anything else to do. You could always build chairs when you didn't have no regular job. I used to get seventy-five cents for a chair back then. Of course that bought a lot back then, too."

With an Old Timer jackknife he began split-

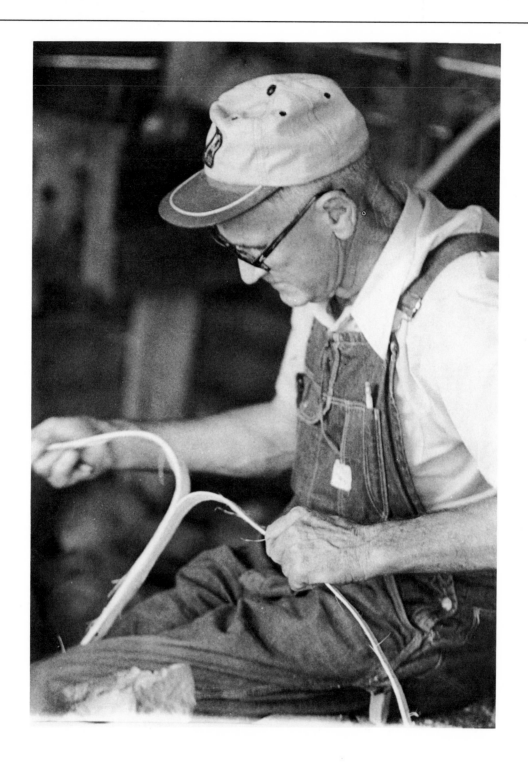

ting out seat bottoms. "Making this twill looks hard. But they's not nothing to it to a person who knows how to do it.

"A lot of people lived completely off it, making chairs. I always logged, carpentered, farmed,

and preached some. I'm retired now, but I took it up again for a pastime and a little income. Guess I'll sell them at trade days around here. I don't imagine a furniture store'd be interested in them. I guess they just use factory stuff.

"These six I made took about a couple of weeks. I'm asking fifteen dollars for each one. You know there's a certain amount of pleasure in making something like this yourself—calling it all back out of memory. I got the pattern off a rocker I made for my wife back when we had our first baby. Sure did. That's what it is, a nursery rocker. That's why it sits this low—and has a little creak in it. Some folks like that."

He sat back on the draw horse and shoved

back his billed fishing cap to wipe his brow. "One nice thing about this trade, people are their own boss. My folks always said they'd rather make chairs than be bossed. Of course I like that too," he said, smiling.

Then Bailey thumped the bottom of a finished rocker and twirled it upside down to show the handiwork underneath the seat. "I tie knots in my white oak splits. That white oak really makes a good chair. Some folks go to just sticking the stray ends down anywhere and you can't tell the difference from looking. But it'll get plumb loose like that and swag down. I tie knots in mine, even though I end up wasting more splits. But I'd rather just do what I do—and do it right."

C. B. Toms

C. B. Toms rested forward with both elbows propped on the counter of his shoe shop, his glasses sliding down his nose, a well-worn felt hat propped comfortably back on the crown of his head. His face wore the look of a man at ease with his world, in no hurry to get anywhere. Through his cracked glasses he squinted amicably at "Ol' Man Cooper, the goat man of Alexander," who was wheezing through his white mustache in friendly small-talk about the pair of shoes Toms had just finished working on.

Mrs. Toms sat quietly to the side, smiling.

Leaning against the wall with a characteristic sly grin on his face, Bill Lowrance, C. B.'s assistant, watched with his one good eye.

Cooper was fumbling with the repaired shoes. "How much yu give me for these shoes?" he asked the gathering.

"Twenty-five cents," said Bill.

"Shoot!" Cooper exploded from beneath his mustache in good-natured disgust, "I just paid fifty cents to fix 'em!"

The group gathered in the shop laughed easily. C. B. wet his bottom lip with his tongue, scratched behind one ear—which threw his hat brim down over his eyes—and chuckled, his laugh rasping like a sharpening file on a rusty saw.

While the main stock and trade of Tom's store was shoe repair, it did a more than adequate business in talk, and talk went cheap. "Not many places you can come to now and just sit and talk," C. B. said. "They're likely to make you buy something." But there were no high-pressure salesmen at Toms's. There were, on the other hand, two church pews and two well-used red metal garden chairs that sat in front of the store. There cracker-barrel chats went on daily from seven-thirty in the morning until five in the evening, when Toms's closed down for another day.

Toms was not what one would call a model Chamber of Commerce member. He was likely to be up on events but reluctant to join in. When asked if he'd been watching the results of that day's downtown sidewalk sale, Toms had an ironic smile. "Ain't been out," he said. He and his cronies seemed more interested in shooting the breeze than in turning a dollar.

The front room of the shop contained no less than five picture calendars, a buck-board wagon seat, an antique sawed-off pistol, a floor fan, a broken candy machine, several mule-harness mirrors, special town license slips from years past, an ancient cash register, a coffee pot, a toaster, bags of repaired shoes (long overdue to be picked up), and a gallon jar of Toms's own honey in a Miracle Whip jug. The floor was finished in four different patterns of linoleum tile, and in the window a decal admonished pedestrians, "You Need a Texas Shine, Boy."

"Too few places let you just come in and talk. They're always making out for you to buy something. Don't want anybody hanging around. Why, shoot, I don't like to go to these new stores. They don't know me and I don't know them. They're just out to get my money. Why, they don't want to talk to me or pass the time-a-day. It's rush, rush, all the time. I tell you, what folks want is to be treated friendly-like, and by-gosh, there aren't many places left where a man can just come in and set a spell."

In the chair beside Bill, Alonzo Doggett, with scythe in hand, nodded in agreement.

C. B. began talking about the old grocery store that used to stand in back of Eagles, where the parking lot is now. "You used to be able to go in there and get anything."

Bill, from his reclining position in one of the garden chairs, added, "Yeah, used to call it Horne's Trash Store, it had so much stuff."

76

old man lived over Main Street. The richest man in the county, I heard tell. Went up there once't. Lived like a hawg.

"Back in the twenties, the square wasn't nothing but a mud hole," he continued. "They had a watering trough out there. I think Martin Greene's got it now over in his backyard. Then, later on, they laid the square in brick. I was just a little boy, but I remember one time a man came through town in one of the first cars. It was a steamer. Must have been one of them Stanley Steamers . . ."

Into the shop strode a distinguished-looking man, with curly gray hair and a proud look about him. Bill saluted the newcomer, who quickly took off his shoes and announced, "Lift it up on this side, will you, Bill." He spoke with a West Indian accent, musically and in staccato bursts.

"Hey, Boss!" the Caribbean native addressed C. B., "Throw me a piece of dat papah." He carefully placed his clean white socks on a newspaper section and sat back to wait for Bill, who ducked into the back of the shop.

The back was the heart of the shop, full of ancient shoe repair machines, draping strings, cords, odd bits of leather, old shoes, nails, and glue drippings. Years of leather glue blackened the floor. The smell was the odor of glue, shoe polish, and leather, and the sound was the reliable putter of the machines. From one corner came the sound of a gospel station, the radio itself almost completely camouflaged by old shoes.

C. B. pulled over a drink carton to stand on and stretched up with both hands to try and get the decrepit ceiling fan to respond, while Bill bent over the cobbler's stand, coughing, squinting, and working around a cigarette with a persistent ash hanging on.

"How ya comin', Chiv.?"

"They used to have chickens back in a coop. Knew of one farmer who sold one hen back three times to them, in the same day," C. B. recollected.

"That was me," crackled Bill. "They bought one hen off'n me three times. I shouldn't have did that, though," he guffawed.

C. B., who was sixty-four, began remembering old days in Forest City. "Once't was an

"Not so good," C. B. muttered. "Must have a bad wahr."

"Put it on fast speed," Bill said, hammering on the shoe. "Gotta take this heel off right here," Bill mused to himself, then called again, "How ya comin', Chiv?"

"Not so good," C. B. grunted.

"We'll fix you some shoes one of these days, George," Bill addressed a visitor. Then abruptly he called out again, "How ya comin', Chiv?"

"Got a bad wahr," C. B. sighed, giving up on the fan.

Bill was finishing the shoe when the West Indian strolled in his white stocking feet into the back of the shop and found another chair to plop down in and another newspaper section to place his feet on. "You didn't build it up too high, Boss?" he asked.

Bill replied, "They're going to be right when I get done with them. They are going to be *right*."

"Yeah, yeah. That what I mean. Sure, sure."

Just then, Otto, with thick glasses, taped cane, two toothpicks in his mouth, and newsboy-style money pouch on his belt, entered and began bartering with the customer over a ragged billfold. C. B. grinned as the two insulted and jawed at each other. He presided over it all with a sort of lordly patience.

There was time for a lunch break with fish sandwiches from the dime store and some home-brewed coffee. Outside on this hot July day the parade of Main Street flowed incessantly by. The floor fan inside fluttered the leaves of the five calendars as the breeze kept the front of the shop cool. C. B., his wife, and Bill Lowrance were silent, keeping cool, and watching the square for something to happen. Something to talk about.

79

Joe Millard

Joe Millard rolled up his sleeves, lashed a stiff apron about him, and began firing up his blacksmith shop. "Ain't nobody doing it now. Nobody's doing nothing now. The country's growing up," he said.

In one of the few remaining smithy shops west of Charlotte, Joe Millard had been blacksmithing for thirty-six years. "Outside the time spent in the Army," he said, "been usin' that hammer."

In his shop everything was as it should have been. The massive anvil stood on a squatty stump in the center of the dirt-floored shop. "That's a walnut anvil block," Joe explained, pointing to where the stump was imbedded in the floor for sturdiness. "I'd rather have post-oak stump, but the one I had for 'bout twenty years was rottin' away," he said, pulling out a plug of tobacco.

The light streamed in through the two open doors on either end of the shed. About the corners were piled old mule shoes, broken wagon wheels, cans of nails, and tools of every sort. Joe's well-worn hammer rested beside the blackened anvil.

With the fire going in the corner, Joe cranked the bellows and the flame shot up through the coal. Using tongs, he placed a plow he was making into the fire and left it to heat. "I make all my own plows. Haven't bought one in thirty years. Make them from old truck springs." He took the plow from the fire and laid it on the anvil.

Picking up the hammer, he began beating out the plow into the desired shape.

"I commenced in '32. To make a long story short, I started this way." He turned the plow and hammered some more. "Old colored man, Ol' Jonas Wilkins, used to be the man to shoe mules and sharpen plows when I was a boy. Some years we could get it done; other years, we couldn't. And when that plow point gets dull, it's killin' on a man and a mule. Need a sharp'un to take the ground.

"First thing I knowed, I was covered up sharpening plows and shoeing. That was thirty years ago. Now everybody uses tractors. Back in those days, though, I shoed ten mules a day. Now when you've done that, you know you've done a day's work. All for one dollar. I can remember some days when I done twelve mules." Joe Millard laughed, remembering he charged just one dollar for all that shoeing. "Now, the nails'll cost that much.

"Back in the thirties, I'd stay pretty busy all summer long on days too wet to be in the fields, sharpening up plows and tightening wagon wheels. Now, nobody does blacksmithing. . . . Now, I'll tell you, there's a Gibson boy down on the Cleghorn road that still does some of this, and Roy McBrayer does some too. But most of it's in the past."

Julius Forney

Julius Forney, almost sixty-four, was gold mining again on the very land he had worked during the thirties when he was a paid laborer for somebody else. Now the land was his. It was the same land on which the Bechtler family had mined their gold in the 1840s. The Bechtlers minted the first gold U.S. one-dollar pieces from 1833 to 1842, and Rutherford County was the nation's leading supplier of coin gold.

"I worked many a night all night long down there," he said, waving to the mossy lips of the cavern, which went straight down seventy feet or more. "There's gold in there, yessir, gold, I'm sayin'." Forney's eyes got a little bigger. "And I oughta know. I've been mining since I was eighteen."

Forney, a sensible man with a steady job in Rutherfordton, didn't have a bad case of gold fever. He just loved mining and couldn't stay away from it any longer. "It's more or less a hobby with me," he explained, walking the couple of acres he recently bought north of Rutherfordton toward Union Mills. " 'Cause I was raised in it. My daddy worked this mine for Miller and Sage Mining Company, and so did I. I took his place as ground foreman in '42 after he died."

He had brought his cousins and their kids out to the mine site that afternoon to show them around. The two younger boys were scampering through the woods, dangerously close to the mine. "Get back, Ron!" Forney scolded. "If you fell in there, you'd never smile again. I don't want to work here all night getting you out of that hole and you not know where you was when you got out." He had an old miner's respect for the shaft.

Forney knelt down by the side of the mine, named Beulah, and pointed down there into the dark. He took off his green faded cap, revealing a thicket of white hair. "Back when I was mining

for Miller and Sage, we had a cave-in. I'll never forget," he remembered, while his cousins and the boys stood by listening intently. "One night late down there my brother-in-law, Russell, and I were down there working. Russell was preaching while he worked. You know, he was pretending that he was a-preachin'. Well, I saw the ground tricklin' down around the timberin', and I told Russell, 'You better get back,' but Russell just went on a-preachin'. And then there was more ground groaning down. I hollered, 'Lookout, Russell!' and grabbed him and pulled him back, and the whole shaft caved in there where he was."

"Good grief!" one of Forney's cousins exclaimed.

"We're going in there again, just as soon as I can get it timbered up," Forney said, taking some maple sprigs to demonstrate how the mine was shored up with wooden braces. "Now, y' see, this timber here braces this 'un."

Forney recalled that the day his father died, "I was working in the mine, and we found a Bechtler one-dollar piece. I guess it was lost back in the slave times—they had slaves working down in that hole then. I sold it to Creed Mitchum for three dollars and fifty cents. Of course, it's worth more than that now."

Forney stopped gold mining when the Second World War started. "We went down to Cleveland County and mined for mica because the government needed it more than gold. I'm just now getting back into it."

He began laying out a row of stones in a little wall on the ground. "This is how the vein runs. This here is the walling," he said, pointing to a smooth-sided quartz piece. "The gold's in here. Carried in iron ore or in quartz ore. Or sulfides. Sulfides carry the gold.

"I messed with this so much I know a good piece of ore when I see it. You take that ore and

you mill it. Divide the ore from the gold and from the sand and rock—you call that tailings. It's like a peach grader. Shakes out the sulfides and the gold catches on the plate—the gold do—'cause it's heavier," Forney said.

"I had that piece of ore with gold plainly visible in it down at the coin show last week at the bank. It came out of this hole here." He held up another piece of rusty-looking ore. From within, like lights from within the rock, minute particles of gold gleamed.

"The real McCoy. It's the real stuff," Forney noted confidently. "You can tell it's not fool's gold. Look here." He took a piece of fool's gold and wet it with some water. "See, it turns whiter the wetter and longer you rub it. But this," he wet the gold sample, "see? It stays just that dull gold glow. Don't turn white. You can wet it all day and it'll never change."

He produced an old battered gold pan, and scooping up some earth from the site, he began washing it around and around in a pool of water. In five minutes, he had reduced it to a fine silt, and there winking from the bottom of the pan was a swatch of heavy ore particles. "This is placer gold mining. And there in that ore, is gold," Forney said. "That's the way they did it out in California. We're not doing it that way here, but I just wanted you to see that to show you how it's done."

He stood up and began walking through the woods, until he came to a collapsing concrete foundation. "This was the old base for the concentrating tables of the Miller and Sage Mining Company," he said. There on the concrete was carved the date 1938. The woods were covered with forty years of leaves and humus.

Scratching around in the leaves, he uncovered part of an old outbuilding. "It's been a long time," he mused. "And I've done many a thing since then. I'd forgotten all this was in here." The old buildings had caved in and decayed. The Bechtlers had died and scattered; none of their progeny was left in these hills. And the mine named Beulah was abandoned and dark. Yet the lure of gold was still strong to this man. He kept going back down into the hole. "I may be losing money, but I love to lose money that way," Forney smiled.

Roscoe Gilbert

Roscoe Gilbert bent over a chestnut nightstand, perfecting some final detail. "One way or the other, I been working with wood all my life. Sawmilling, buildin' houses, cabinet makin' and furniture." The craftsman's smile was permanent and genuine. Now eighty-eight, he had been handcrafting furniture for seventy-two years. Everyday he went to his woodworking shop in Green Hill, where he followed his craft, pegging and dovetailing as though nothing had changed in the art of fine furniture making since the turn of the century, when he began.

"It was sort of in the family, y'see. My father was what you'd call a gunsmith and a right good blacksmith too. I just kept working at it. Bought my first set of tools for eight dollars and built my first piece of furniture—a little ole' table—in 1903. Did it with just my brace and bit. Whittled out the dowels myself and dressed the lumber with my hand plane," he grinned.

His much-wrinkled face carried a patina of wood dust, and he coughed occasionally from the powdery sawdust. Gripping his pencil firmly in his mouth, he moved confidently about the shop from tool to tool, planing a door, gluing the molding, attaching the hinges, and so forth, in orderly progression.

"I made my own machines. Instead of buying 'em I just made 'em." That included a circular mortice saw for frames, special bits and drills for dowels and wooden pegging, a special planer, and turning machines complete with turning chisels that Roscoe crafted to his own liking. "You know, it takes a little practice to do this," he said with a laugh.

"When I ran my cabinet shop down in Forest City, I got to be known as the best cabinetmaker

in the county. But this lady she came to me and wanted those ol' cheap cabinets. I said to her, I says, 'Lady, hit takes just as much labor to build them ol' sorry cabinets as it does to build my good 'uns.' I don't build them kind, I tol' her." Straightening up, he said sternly, "I don't build no kind but the good 'uns."

Then he was laughing again to himself. "Now where did I put that little poke full of hinges?"

Roscoe's wife Lola appeared at the shop's door, holding on to her walking stick. Two tiny grizzled dogs wandered in beneath her feet and plopped down in sunlighted splotches of warm wood chips. "His son Arnold holpt him build this shop fifteen years ago," she related, as she fingered a piece of chestnut and watched Roscoe peg the leg of a one-hundred-and-fifty-year-old walnut secretary he was repairing. "There's not nobody but him that still pegs furniture. Glue and nails couldn'ta holt what he pegs," she said proudly.

He was working on the last of three bedroom suites made from wormy chestnut. The completed dresser sat in one corner of the shop awaiting the two nightstands. "Chestnut is just about the best wood to work there are. When the blight killed it back, the wood fell and was cut. The wood is so acidy that nothing can rot it. Only the worms can get in. So you can still find up the woods huge logs fallen for thirty years covered with moss. Sink your ax into one and it'll still be sound as a dollar.

"Something I build out of chestnut will be good one hundred years from now if any type of good care is took of it at all. Why, that wood'll make the prettiest boards ever you looked at. Oak and chestnut, you might say, are brothers, but I like chestnut better to work with because it splits so nicely."

Roscoe stood beside the chestnut dresser and caressed the counter top. "Well, yes, it does

take a little doin'," he chuckled with amusement. Arching one eyebrow and clapping his hands roughly, making wood-dust motes dance in the sunshafts, he laughed again, "Y'know, there's a whole lotta art to it."

Ervin Hale Barnette

Cane in one hand and gas can in the other, Ervin Hale Barnette trudged steadily up the steep incline of the old Marion Road outside of Rutherfordton. Over the top of his spectacles he surveyed the road shoulder with one good eye. He was making the two-hundred-yard trek to buy gas for his hand tractor.

"Used to be a time when I'd stand on the tracks in front of a train going forty miles per hour and put out one leg and jump aboard the front of the cow-catcher and think nothin' of it," he said. Barnette's life-style was considerably quieter now than it had been in those halcyon days, but even at ninety he still managed to put a garden in every year. And he had packed the experiences of three lifetimes into those years.

He prospected for gold in British Columbia, Alaska, and Mexico, railroaded in all forty-eight

states, and appeared as a bit player in fourteen Hollywood movies during the thirties. He barely escaped from train wrecks, led pack trains into the snowy wilderness of the Sierra Nevadas near the turn of the century, and sold books and Bibles. And he managed to do some farming.

"Was raised up in Kentucky," he related. "Went to school my first day and got whipped. Big raw-boned man of a teacher broke a big ruler over me 'cause I wouldn't sit next to a boy and look on with him in reading. The boy was covered with lice. Naturally, I didn't much want to sit there and share a seat.

"That teacher came back and jerked me up by the collar and whupped me. Broke that big ruler with its brass rail all to pieces. At recess I slipped off and got the boat across the back-water river of the Ohio and headed for home. When my older brother, a big eighteen-year-old, saw me, he says, 'I believe I need some more education!'

"So the next day he went to school with me, carried a newspaper rolled up in his back pocket, and he sat at the very back of the class. Funny thing, but the teacher didn't pay too much attention to me all day. Guess he was payin' attention to my brother.

"My brother finally chewed up a big wad of paper, and when he got it right, he let sail. That big teacher looked back there and hollered, 'Boy, you do that again, and I'll come back there and give you the whipping of your life.'

"Brother didn't say anything. Just took that newspaper out, took a big chaw off it, and got it right, and let sail with a big wad again.

"Wellsir, that teacher came flying down the rows, and my brother jumps up to meet him, and they commenced to goin' at it. I thought they must have fought for fifteen or twenty minutes—but maybe it wasn't that long—when my brother knocked the big man down. He got up, and my brother knocked him down again. This teacher, who was a big man, started to get up again, and my brother says, 'If'n you get up again, Man, I'll give you my boot.' Then my brother said to me, 'Come on, let's go home,' and we left. So I didn't have much of a chance after that with education. Got about as far as the fourth grade altogether.

"When I was between twelve and thirteen, I ran away from home to fight in the Spanish-American war. I aimed to go to join up with the Third Kentucky Regiment musterin' down in Chickamauga Park, Georgia. Me 'n this other feller. Barefoot all the way from Richmond County, Kentucky, to fight the Spaniards.

"But when we got to the camp, the captain saw we were too young. Told us the general was away in Chattanooga for the night an' seein' as how it was dark, we could both spend the night in the general's big sleeping bag.

"Well, the general, he came back at three A.M. and found us two boys in his sleeping bag. He pulled us out and gave us a working over with his riding whip. Sure did," Barnett laughed. "We lit out of there and slunk around camp 'til morning.

"The next day, the captain told us he got a letter from my father wanting to know where we were. I know he was lying, but I went on home anyway when I saw they wasn't gonna let us join up on account of us being too young.

"Me 'n my partner was riding home in one of those blind freight cars. We had heard that the conductor would throw people off the train if he caught 'em freeloadin'. Well, he came through that door, and I was so addled I jumped off the train going sixty miles an hour across a trestle. Somehow I jumped out at a cinderfill between the two bridges and rolled down the 'bankment into a briar patch. I was plumb lucky, I knew.

"They stopped the train and backed her up, hollering, 'You all right down there. . . ?'

"I just stayed lying in the briar patch. 'I'm down here, and I'm all right. You just go on,' I hollered back.

"My partner got off to come down and see about me, and the train went on. We walked to the next depot and was sitting there on some ties when that same train came back by in the other direction. The conductor spotted us and asked, 'You the boys who jumped off the train? Well, son, you're mighty lucky to be alive today. Ten feet either way and it'd have been your end,' he told me, and I knew he was right."

Barnette went home and began working on the pump stations for the steam engines in the summer of 1896. At fourteen he began firing engines and by eighteen he qualified as a full-fledged steam locomotive engineer. "On my first day when I got the orders to take a train out, I went to my father, a railroad man, to ask to borrow his watch. I was surprised as anyone about getting the assignment. But Dad just laughed. He was proud, I guess. 'You a hulluva lookin' engineer,' he grinned at me."

By the time Barnette was twenty, he had already worked two years as an engineer. He decided to go to the St. Louis World's Fair of 1903. "In 1903 it seems all the conductors and engineers in the country got it in their mind to go to St. Louis for the World's Fair. You'll remember that song, 'Meet Me in St. Louie, Louie'—

it came out of that time. Well, I went there too. Had it in my mind to get me a job in East St. Louis at the trainyard. It's the biggest in the country, and I figgered that'd be something to tell the boys back home.

"Well, I hadn't been working there but three days when the wreck happened. It was on a steep grade, and I was in charge of fourteen cars coming through the switchin' yard. I was riding a-top the foremost car so I could see what was happening up ahead. Well, I saw this old drunk brakeman by the side of the track and he sang out, 'Have a looooong ride!'" Barnett threw his head back and imitated the inebriated railman.

"Well, Sir, I looked out there, and there in front of us was eight sand cars sitting right in our way. Well, we were coming along at a goodly clip, and I was afraid if I stayed on top of the lead car, I'd be killed for sure, but I daren't jump to the side either, for fear of being crushed in the wreck.

"I took it in my mind to jump into the first sand car before the two trains hit. So just at the last moment I jumped. Now, back then they had wooden sand cars, so that when I landed in the sand car, and the train I had been on hit the cars, why, the bottom of the sand car fell out and if you can imagine swimming in sand, well, that's what I did.

"All that sand, and me too, we fell through the bottom of the wooden floor base and somehow landed on the track beneath. How I escaped being crushed by the wheels I never will know. Must have landed on the track, just beneath the wheels and barely escaped being killed.

"When I came to, I couldn't see, couldn't hear, and couldn't talk. Ears, nose, mouth, and eyes full of sand. I remember I couldn't find my hat, but I didn't care. I lit out of there as fast as I could go. Went back to my room to clean up, and didn't tell nobody about what had happened.

"Well, I went back in three days, and the foreman saw me and says, 'Barnette, we thought you was dead. We've been scratching around in that sand for three days looking for you. All we found was your hat. It's up in the shanty.' Then he said to me, 'You are coming back to work aren't you?'

"I told him, 'Why, hello, no. All I want is my money and my hat!' and I cleared out of there for good.

"A year later I went to Cincinnati. Never forget that. Got robbed there. Had eighty-five dollars in my overcoat pocket and just a little change in my pockets. The thieves took everything, but I still had my coat on. When they said, 'Give us your coat,' that's when I started crying," Barnette play-acted, rocking back on the couch, and crying crocodile tears. "Please, you've taken all my worldly possessions," he moaned. "And here it's dead of winter and you want to take my old ratty overcoat and leave me to freeze."

"Well, Sir, those thieves kicked me good in the bottom side and said, 'Well, all right, and get going.' I'll say that was the sweetest kick I've ever had."

Barnette began touring the nation as a boomer sometime after that. A boomer, he said, was a roving railroadman, someone who could step in on any road and pick up the job—whether it was braking, firing, switching, or engineering. He did that in almost every state.

By 1900 he had worked his way to British Columbia, working with the Canadian Pacific Railroad. He met and married his wife, Alice, there that same year. But gold pickings were slim so they moved south to the states in 1913.

"Hallelujah!" Barnette cried. "I was glad to be back. I told Alice to stay in San Francisco with forty dollars and come when I sent for her, and I took ten dollars and went out looking for work. Went down to the San Joachin Valley,

where they had a road, and went to working there. I recall when I was conductor there was a derailment and they tried three different times to get the engine back on the track.

"The railroad superintendent was watching, and I crawled under the train and adjusted the frogs the way I knew they should be and then told them to start 'er up. Well, the train just jumped back on the track and the superintendent was grinning from ear to ear. That's when they found that 'that Barnette kid' was an engineer."

Barnette once hauled a whole trainload of silver to Monterrey when he was working in 1923 in "old Mexico" on the Mexican Central.

While there, he caught blood poisoning, and he had to buck every rule in the book to save his life. "In old Mexico, they've got this rule that a train can't move without a conductor. Well, I had my fireman, and I was the engineer. In the states that's all you need. And I couldn't get a conductor until that evening. And by then I might be dead.

"I told the dispatcher I had to get back to Torreón right away to see the doctor because I had blood poisoning. But they wouldn't let me come without a conductor. I told that man, I'm comin' anyway. If I don't, it'll mean the life of me.

"So they let me go, and the moment I got to town and found the doctor, I saw the railroad superintendent and train master walk in. 'I think I've got blood poisoning,' I told the doctor. He looked at my arm and said, 'I think so, too,' and those two men just never said a thing, but just walked out of the office. If'n I'd been wrong, it would have been a bad time for me, I'll tell you."

He returned to America and to California where, "I quit railroadin' about fifteen or sixteen times," he said with a grin. In the late twenties he began leading pack trains into the mountains near Huntington Lake in the Sierras.

"Most every Hollywood movie shot in that area hired out my men and horses. They had an agreement with me that they could use me in any little bit part they needed, so I was in about fourteen motion pictures from '27 on through the thirties. Worked with Bruce Gordon, Ruthe Roland, Bessie Love, and Bill Rogers.

"One time I had to carry Ruthe Roland out of a house a-fire. I guess that was my biggest thrill. Ruthe, she was a sweet girl, but could shoot craps with the best of us, down on her knees and growling, 'Come on, seven!'" he grinned.

Barnette finally moved to North Carolina in 1950 to a farm in the east near Winterhaven. "When it rained, the water stood twelve inches on my place. Kids used to say, 'Let's go swimming in Barnette's lake.' They meant my yard." Through a friend the Barnettes heard about Rutherfordton and moved there.

"1948 was the last time I was sick," he said. "If'n I hadn'ta worked so hard, I'd been dead long ago. When you shovel coal as a fireman at sixteen for twenty-four hours a day, then you've done a man's work."

But he had lost an eye when a bug hit him in his left eye as he was leaning out the window of the engine years ago. And his eighty-two-year-old wife's health wasn't as strong as it had been. So Barnette wanted finally to return to his native Richmond County, Kentucky, home. "There, we've got family," he said, patting the "For Sale" sign in front of his place on the old Marion Road. "I guess after ninety years I'm ready to go home."

Frank King

Frank King made baskets the old way—from hand-split white-oak strips. He fashioned them into clothes hampers, wood baskets, and garden baskets ranging in size from quart to bushel. "My daddy showed me how to build a basket when I was a little boy, so I ran out in the woods and got my materials," Frank laughed, as he did often. "Seems like that's all I can do now. Guess I've been making baskets and cane-bottoming chairs now for 'bout seventy-five years. Well I do say," Frank sang in a cheery soprano giggle. "There's all times something what's gotta be gwine on."

He began with the wood; white oak was best. He went to the woods and cut the small saplings, then trimmed them down with an ax and split them into long white strips with a hunting knife and maul at his work shed. Finally, he used a drawknife to fashion the thin basket strips.

The shed was Frank's studio. Tools, bits of iron, chains, and busted plow points were jumbled about on the weather-board walls. The hard-packed earth floor was covered with oak shavings, and a large much-scarred chopping block took up one corner.

The faded appearance of his overalls, flannel shirt, and floppy Irish tweed hat formed a sharp contrast to his eyes, which were still sharp and quick to laugh.

He practically did a jig when he told of a man who ordered three hundred dollars worth of baskets. "Mister! I don't know how long it'll take me," he had told him. "Three hunnerd dollahs worth—well, I do say." He waggled his head and scratched a grey stubble with one massive hand in mock amazement.

"There's a terrible call for 'em," he said, nodding toward a pile of baskets in the corner of his back porch. "I guess I'm close to around being the last one. People call me from Asheville and Greenville—all over."

Taking a handful of finely dressed splits that

he had prepared the day before with the draw-knife, Frank laid out a star pattern on a stool and began to build a basket. With a hank of cane, he started weaving in and out, in and out, making the basket's base.

"My pappy, who taught me, used to make baskets for other people around the farm. Back then he thought fifty cents for one was big money. You know, money was *money* them days.

"We used to tend right smart of land in them days. Plowed with oxen. Pappy and them'd farm and we allus had plenty to eat—sech as it was. I believe we ate better than we do now. Had veg'tables and all like that, and home-grown meat.

"Folks thought if you hadn't broke up the land by the first of February, that you were behind. I do love to farm. Want to put out an early roastin' ear patch myself this year, you know.

" I 'member I was thirteen when the nineteenth century went out and the twentieth commenced. I was right up there at an old wooden store up 'ahr." he waved northward. "We were kinda confounded, wonderin' how we'd figger out the date of the year with this new nineteen hunnerd thing-a-ma-do. That's what we wanted to know. Well," Frank laughed at himself, "hit's very reasonable if you know how to work it—and it all worked out."

His large nimble fingers worked ceaselessly as he turned the basket in his hands and looped the splits through the maze of ribs. He had wet the splits beforehand to limber them up. "If ye don't," he advised, "they'll break on account of its being dry."

He began talking about the grim days of slavery that were his parents' heritage. "Tough times back then." Frank bent close and scowled at the developing basket's pattern. "My pappy tol' me how he had to plow bareheaded and without shoes—with hit a snowin'. Yeah. Tough times,

102

tough times," he said, jamming the hunting knife into the chopping block.

"I recall my father tellin' me he was a slave for a man named King back up near Hendersonville County before the war come and freed the colored people. He tol' me they'd fill up a horse or a hog trough and have to get down all together and eat outen that. Had to pray out from under that. Had to pray and trust the Lord to free 'em. We've had it tough alright." He shook his head.

"My mother belonged to an old white man back around Forest City. In slavery times colored folks had to do what the man said. My mother's father was a white man. That's how come I'm all mixed up," he said, indicating his light skin.

"It's hurting to think about it—but when my daddy passed, he was ninety-three and I was holding his hand. Holding it right there when he passed." Frank's voice choked with emotion, and he fought to retain control. "But . . . but just before he passed he said, 'Howdy, Mama. Howdy, Mama. . . . They sold you away from me in slavery.'" Frank paused for a deep breath. "He musta seed her through the spirits. He said, 'Howdy, Mama. Howdy.'"

The star of white-oak splits in Frank King's hands now elbowed upward, and a framework of spaced runners threaded in and out. Turning away from his memories, Frank said gayly, "Boys, I'll have you a little egg basket, won't I."

Quiet for a time, Frank worked on in thought, stopped, put down the almost finished basket and preached. "I used to not believe. Said I didn't have the sense. But I was a-walkin' down that road yonder where's the red clay cut and I had a vision. I had this vision of a man come down straight outa the sky and he said to me, 'Frank, you can't say you don't have the sense to believe. Go read Paul's letter to the Corinthians.'

"Ever since that time I've been a different man. The Bible says obey your mother and

father and your days shall be long. It also says to obey your father in heaven," he said, pointing up with one hand, "and things'll go well with you afterwards.

"The Bible says to wait on the Lord. *Wait* on Him. People won't do like that. People want to go the doctor and pay big money—and die just the same. Instead of studyin' on how to get ready to die, people studyin' on gettin' rich.

"I'm not able to get up and stir around in the fields like I used to. Seems like I've got to be doing something or else, Lordamercy, we'll perish. Uh-huh!"

All the while Frank's big hands were delicately pushing and shoving the moistened thin strips of wood into place. Finally, he exploded with a "Waaah-ooh! That's a cute little ol' thing." Holding up the basket for final approval, he expressed what most artists must feel but seldom put so succinctly when a good job is well done. He screwed up his face and concluded, "Whooo-peee!"

Aunt Nan Harrill

When ninety-one-year-old Aunt Nan Harrill was not feeling well, she loved nothing better than for John Johnson to come around with his tall tales, small talk, and banjo picking. Then when conversation had subsided maybe John and Celestia Blanton, who stayed with Aunt Nan, would play some well-worn sacred number.

Aunt Nan used to play the banjo herself, but "m' hands quit on me," she said. But if John insisted—and even went so far as to set the five-string in the white-haired matriarch's lap, then the fingers would play as if they had minds of their own.

She lived just above the Puzzle Creek Bridge in a farmhouse that was the core of what had been a thriving farm. Now, three log outbuildings and a spacious silvered barn huddled under giant oaks.

Aunt Nan sat rocking in her parlor before a roaring Perfection oil stove, her white hair tied back in a bun. She wore a black sweater, a white cotton apron, a faded print dress, and white cotton socks and slippers. Bending toward the stove, she rocked there slowly, hands clasped like granny knots, rocking in cadence with the old clock that was noisly marking time on the wall.

Her late husband, Shufford ("We called him Shoop—a short name."), was a carpenter. John recalled how "Shoop used to get up before sunup and walk every day to Henrietta and help build that mill and then walk all the way back. I heard him tell it many a time. I'm satisfied it's ever' bit of eight miles from here to Henrietta Mill. Yessir."

Above Aunt Nan's head hung an ancient oval photograph of her parents. The picture hung at least six feet off the ground. With a teasing look, Aunt Nan explained, "Ol' John put that picture way up there on the wall. John was here when we moved. John's high up, you know. He's the one

that hung that picture so high up there I can't get to it to rub the dust off. That's my ma 'n' pa, Perry and Susan Hardin.

"I's raised over Piney Ridge way. Adaville on down toward Harris. I ain't a-been back in there for a long time. All that new stuff's come up since I been over in there. I never got to the fifth grade. I went to a free school down on Piney Ridge. Charles Moore used to teach it way back yonder. We'd just fight and scratch and tell tales. Dip snuff and spit. One thing and another.

"Pa played a fiddle a little ways. The brothers had a banjer, and they'd hide it from me when they'd go off. But I'd find it, and that's how I learnt the banjer. When they saw I was good, they'd let me join in. But I can't play no more. My fingers won't let me.

"I do more talking than anything else. That's all I can do. I can't walk much hardly at all. The doctor tol' me I was gonna be deaf. 'Well,' I said, 'If I'm gonna be deaf, I'd rather have my eyes.' Well, I can't see good, and I can't hear good, and I can't walk—but I can *talk*, and I can *eat*, and I'm a-goin' on ninety-two year old. Huh? It's true. The 17th of September.

"'Well, how old are you?' somebody asked me. And I said I'm going on ninety-two. And he said, 'I won't live to be that old.' And I said, 'You will if you work hard enough, sir.'

"I've worked hard all my life. I've done more work than any two men in the country, I guess. I done everything on the farm except cut wheat and go in the mud ditch. I could plow, I could plant corn with a planter, and I could keep up with a five-dollar man, cutting wheat and throwing down the bundle. Used to, way back, they'd charge five dollars to cut wheat all day. I could stay right behind him.

"I've had a tough time of it. But nobody bothers us much. Nobody coming around at night. They're scared of me. Well, they oughta

be. I tol' 'em I'd shoot 'em. And if I didn't shoot 'em, I tol' 'em I had a walkin' stick and I'd whup the fahr outa 'em. Yeah. A walkin' stick. I'd use that on 'em when they come to the door if I don't like the looks of 'em.

"Lordamercy. That ol' woman—why, everybody in the country knows me, I reckon. Might near. And I ain't never had a fuss with anybody around in the country. No racket. And I don't want one.

"I been 'round here a long time. Ninety-one goin' on ninety-two. I was eleven months old when the big earthquake come in Charleston. You don't recollect that, but you've heard folks talk about it. Well, now, I was eleven months old and Pa run outa doors and everything got to rattlin' and shakin' in the house and scared him. He run out the door and looked around. The dog's a-barkin' and everybody was a-hollerin'. He hollered back in the house and says, 'Old woman, get up that young'un. Let's go on to your mother's,' says, 'It's the end of time.' And she started out to see what he'd had to say, and when she went out I commenced to cryin'. And she said she looked around out there and looked up at the stars and said, 'Why, Perry, the stars is shinin'. It ain't no end of time.' And she went back to me. I was crying. I was eleven months old. That was in 1886. Eleven months old when that big earthquake come.

"You can count back and see how old I am. Old ain't good, but you can't find nobody to say nothin' 'gainst me—'cept just quare and can't see. I'll never forget that, long as there's breath in me. It was a powerful shake.

"That 'tater house my husband built, and I helped build it. We used to have that thing full of 'taters. Used to have all our own meat in that log smokehouse. That 'tater house was full of a thousand bushel of 'taters—John knows we raised 'taters—and we had all our own meat, corn, flour, and everything. Didn't have to buy nothin' but sugar and coffee. That's right. That's ol'-timey stuff now, feller. Have all the ham meat I wanted. Oh, mercy. Smoked ham and big ol' pans of that ol' liver mush and chicken—I had the woods full of chickens—and get up eggs, and two milk cows, and go to the field every day and come back and milk two cows and churn and sold milk and eggs and butter every week—that's what I done. Man, I was smart. John knows me. I'm not tellin' no lies. Yessir, I've sit out there under that oak tree and counted 'tater slips all day long, fifty in a bunch, tied, and lay 'em down. And count as much as fifteen hunnerd. And we'd ship 'em up to Spruce Pine. I used to be a lot of help. But I ain't no count now. I've had a hard life, but I've been around, feller."

Victor Logan

The light entered the workshop from one dusty window and fell on Victor Logan, playing in and about the grooves and wrinkles of his face as he bent patiently over a piece of wood on the workbench.

The only sound in the shop was the scraping of Logan's chisel on the curly maple. The smell was of wood dust and musty oldness. High on the dark shelves there were mysterious and wonderful boxes tied meticulously with strings and labeled for nails, bolts, and screws. Well-used and worn tools of the trade lay in disarray.

On a clothesline in one corner two violins hung, awaiting the final touch of the master. Logan was a master craftsman, a violin maker for more than forty years.

"I've never sold one," he said, tightening the strings on one of his violins. "Not that I haven't had offers. I just do it for fun, and besides, I like having them just hanging around here."

His handsome red-headed wife stood outside the shop and gazed affectionately at her husband. "He's got the gift," she said. "He just loves to work with his hands."

He never had any formal music training, but he taught himself and now "plays anything he can get his hands on." He is even the church organist at Bostic Presbyterian.

"I just made myself learn it as a boy," he said. "I was the oldest of the Logan boys on our farm out near Washburn's Store. We took up music because there was no way to get into Forest City for picture shows. We just picked it up to keep ourselves entertained.

"I built my first violin in 1932. I had nothing to copy 'cause we farm boys had no money like

that. So I borrowed one and built mine just by guess, and when it was done, well, it came out pretty close to the real thing," he said, dusting off the front piece of the violin he was working on.

Violin makers, he explained, build their instruments to the model of the ones Stradivari built over three hundred years ago. "That Italian was the one that first worked out the design for the best violin. I believe he lived between 1600 and 1700. He lived to be ninety-something, and built eleven thousand violins in all. They say one half of them were really good. And they claim there are just a few left today and most of them are in museums.

"Lotta people put 'Stradivarius' on their label inside the violin. But they should put that it's a copy of his model. It's the standard violin we all go by." And then he chuckled, "They have big fine machines that can copy a Stradivarius perfectly, but it just doesn't have the tone."

Logan used only old wood and hand tools, just as Stradivari did. Time in plentiful amounts and patience were other shared ingredients. "I'd say it takes me about a year to build a violin," he explained, picking up his favorite. "I built this one in 1955. Started on Mrs. Logan's birthday, October 1. Not on purpose, just happened that way. And it was finished exactly a year to the day later.

"Oh, you've got to let that glue dry and the varnish set up, not to mention all the chiseling and carving. I can't work out here in the summertime, it gets so awfully hot, and you can't glue or varnish out here in the wintertime, so I don't rush things."

His strong, roughened hands turned an un-

finished violin back over and over, as he inspected the work. "You take a three-quarter-inch piece of good wood, birch and curly maple are the best, and then chisel it out." He indicated his tools. "I made my own tools. Don't have any machinery like regular violin makers." He had chisels he had made out of old files and mounted on homemade wooden handles.

"This violin, one of my favorites, came from a maple that stood up on the old Murray place on Cherry Mountain. The wood is important as it helps control tone, and tone is the thing you work for," Logan said. "That's the thing that counts. And you never know 'til you've strung up the violin how it'll sound. No two violins sound alike. It might be soft and mellow or loud and shrill like

an old-time dance fiddler would like." Tone, Logan said, was a very elusive thing. Old wood and other variables, such as where the wood came from and what type it was, controlled the sound of the violin or fiddle.

He pointed through the curving F-holes of the violin to a pencil-thin pole about an inch high bracing the front and back of the violin. "Now that's the sound post. It's as important in determining the sound as anything. It vibrates and carries the vibration from the top to the bottom. You stick it in the F-holes and nudge it around 'til you get it right. Then again, the F-holes are important too, as they let the tone through," Logan noted.

The detailed work that went into a violin or

fiddle was excruciating. There were seventy-eight pieces in a violin. He made the front, back, sides (bouts), neck, and the headpiece. He even put in purfling, the tiny wood inlay around the violin's border, which demanded exact tooling. Logan had completed fourteen violins, including one viola, and a dulcimer, which he had made after seeing one in the mountains. "I took one look at it and come home and built me one, too."

He was slow to admit he could even play the violin, but finally picked up his favorite, tuned it carefully, and tucked it under his chin. His bow sawed across the strings, and the strains of "Christ the Lord Is Risen Today" filled the workshop. He finished that piece and then went right into "In the Sweet By and By."

Then he stopped to explain the difference beween a violin and a fiddle. "Violin people are a bunch of people proud of themselves and what they can do. A violinist is a man who has been trained and who has studied music. A fiddle—why, a fellow just picks it up and plays it by ear. They're the same instrument exactly. It's just how you play it that makes the difference."

And so Victor Logan, violinist and violin maker, became Victor Logan, old-time fiddler. He let his right foot tap the tempo to the sprightly "Soldier's Joy," a haunting melody reminiscent of a highland bagpipe fling. His fingers flew like the feet of the dancers he might have been imagining while he played the fiddle he had patiently built with his own hands years before—not for money, not for fame or glory, but, as he said, "just because I love the music."

E. B. Hyder

E. B. Hyder of Green Hill had been a nursery-man for over fifty years. He started Green Hill Nursery in 1928. Not the best period to go into business for oneself, but he prospered in spite of the times. "I made more money under Hoover than I did under any other president. The Depression didn't bother me half as much as things do now. Aw, it takes so much to buy things now. It takes a tow sack full now."

His floral handiwork was spread all over Rutherford County. He recalled setting out "all them maples and shrubs around Spindale for Ivory Cowan in the thirties." In his side yard bloomed the first flowering tree each spring. "Dr. Biggs—he's dead now—he brought the parent tree back from England for the Rutherfordton Hospital. 'Don't harm it,' they told me. 'Be real careful,' when I was putting it out near the hospital. But a little rooted section of a sprig fell off, and I came home and planted it. That was back in the thirties, too. Now I believe they've moved around the hospital and destroyed that tree. Star magnolia, that's what it is. Smells good, too."

The great-grandson of a full-blooded Cherokee, the eighty-six-year-old Hyder learned to tend plants in his native Henderson County. He courted the future Mrs. Hyder and, "Doggone if we didn't get married" sixty-four years before. "I liked this section here so I found me a little piece of land on the road and put up my little nursery. And I built me my house all by my lone self."

Hyder mixed nursery work with rock masonry and carpentry. He claimed that he had built forty-eight houses and twenty-five chimneys. One of the toughest jobs was laying the river-rock house on North Washington Street in Rutherfordton. Built in the thirties, it took him eight months of stacking round Black Mountain river rock. "Now, that's a job," Hyder insisted with a wag of eyebrows.

In front of the nursery on the highway a peel-ing, chipped, once green and white sign hung, faded by fifty years of weathering. It wasn't much advertising, but Hyder needed little help there. Trees, daffodils, and shrubs dotted the sunny hillside around Hyder's modest brick home, outbuildings, chicken coop, and pen. Ducks and chickens scratched in the dirt driveway. A neighborhood turkey gobbled, and Hyder's roosters responded with their cockle-doodle-doos. Making his rounds, the old man chuckled at that. "Ha! That makes a feller feel like he's gettin' *young* again—t'hear them old roosters crow. I like to hear that of a mornin'."

From shrubs to chickens ("Get six eggs a day.") to greenhouse, Hyder moved with a steady purposeful shuffle. A "propigatin' house" covered his small rooted cuttings. A heavy-coated pony grazed in a corral that featured a white-blooming plum tree in its center.

A small garden already showed onions, cabbage, and potatoes. "Corn, beans, cucumbers, and I don't know whatever" were still to come. He planted by the signs ("Plant yer pertaters on the dark nights."), still holding on to "the old sayings of the old people." "I kindy keep up what my daddy did, and he planted his garden by the signs, so I do too," he said.

Trees he had set out fifty years before towered over the nursery: pines tall and straight, swaying in the spring breeze, and maples frilly with new growth. "They're a-fixin' to bloom is what they're a-fixin' to do," Hyder observed with a keen eye. One of his favorite trees was the Cunningham fir, a strange prickly evergreen. The tree was nick-named the "monkey pine," supposedly, he said, because, "Them things is so sticky, a monkey can't even climb 'em. They say, but I don't know, 'cause I never seen one try."

Hyder said he owed his longevity to tough stock. "My people, they were all long-lifed. Had uncles that lived to be a hundred and a hundred

and three. Ain't nobody that can keep up with me yet. I can climb a hill quicker'n any man still. And I don't ever forget things. Just tell me what you want here and how many and come back the next day and I'll be around here som'ers and I'll remember.

"I work every day—no matter what the weather. I can always find something to do. Tend to my chickens, tend to my pony, tend to the house cleanin' and cookin', tend to my wife— hardnin' of the arteries y'know." Hooking his fingers into his overall shoulder straps, he said with conviction, "I got to have something to do. I got to keep *moving*. I can't sit down."

L. L. Moore

The door opened suddenly, revealing the sparkly eyed veteran railroadman L. L. Moore, with red nose, red flannel shirt, and a full brush of white hair. He seemed poised to spring from the hallway. Instead he turned with a twist. "Wanna know something about ol'-time railroad days, do you? Well, hard work never hurt nobody. Cause if it did, I'd be dead a long time ago," he announced in his sandpaper voice.

He led the way through the darkened rooms of the converted schoolhouse that he lived in to a warmly lighted study. There he sat in his favorite chair, surrounded by a floor lamp, a Quaker furnace, and a 1920-vintage table radio. Moore, the dean of area railroad men, said that he'd be eighty-nine in February and that he had spent forty-eight of those years working on the railroad. He retired at seventy-four after being the head inspector at Bostic Yard since 1910.

"I was raised up in North Wilkesboro. Father had a farm, but I thought that was a little slow, so I went off to West Virginia and worked in a coal mine for a year. When I got tired of that I went in logging. Was a lumberjack in West Virginia, Tennessee, and Kentucky, but the pay wasn't what I needed. Friend got me a job in Bluefield with the N & W long about 1906 as a car repairman. Shoot, I didn't know a boxcar from a flatcar, but the friend that got me the job told them I was an experienced man, so I got top pay—twenty cents an hour.

"When the Clinchfield opened in 1908, I went down to Johnson City. They moved to Erwin, and I went with them and stayed that winter. Then the boss came along and asked how would I like to come to Bostic. That was long about 1910. I been here ever since.

"I been retired fourteen years. I had it all planned out. I would do nothing but fish. Well," he grinned and waved toward the next room, "I got that rod and reel and the line's never gotten wet. I stay busy with my garden all the time.

"It's been a pretty rough life. Used to work a twelve-to-eighteen-hour day, seven days a week, 365 days a year, and 366 days on leap year. I was on salary, so I'd work all the time. After the men on hour went home, I'd be working on into the night. Believe me, it was work too. Cars broke down, and they were those old weak wooden cars."

He stopped and pulled out some old photos of railroad crews and trains. The men were standing like statues cast in bronze, their faces solemn. "Here's the little shanty we all stayed in at Bostic Yard. And here's an old Mellet. They were a compound engine, French design, I think. And here's one of a wreck down east of Bostic, long about 1915. Killed two men, Rod Greene, the engineer, and his fireman, Dooley. The second engine went when a bridge went out. The first engine escaped. Old Man Walt Lindsey was in it. He wasn't killed. His fireman, a colored fellow, he jumped and escaped. That had the road tied up good. People came in wagons and on mules for miles around to see that wreck. It was a mess, that one.

"Yessir, it was a woolly business then—and it still is—but not like it used to be. Everything's changed now. It all changed after the government took over the railroad after World War One. Up until then, I had been working twelve to eighteen hours a day for ninety dollars a month. But after that government man, McAdoo, took over, they put us all on eight-hour days. I felt like I hadn't done nothing. It was all leisure, yet they 'bout doubled our pay and gave us time and a half. We had it good then—rested two-thirds of the time and made twice as much. Before then I never had time to do things like go to a baseball game. After that, I never missed one around here."

When he retired, his son stepped into his job.

"I was pretty worried at first, but I'll tell you, I watched him pretty close. But he did a better job than I did.

"I go every so often down to the yard, but it's changed so much. They don't have the coal tipple water-stand pipe or the turntable. I been thinking about riding that old Clinchfield steamer, but it wouldn't be too much excitement for me. I'd know exactly what they'd be doing the whole way."

His face broke into a jolly laugh, and he rocked back in his chair as another story came to mind. "I remember Old 500, the first Mellet engine we had. Ol' Jim Little was the engineer. Well, down in the north end of the yard it and a coal train got mixed up and hit face-on. Jim jumped off before she hit, and he went running down the embankment into the river. He said he looked back up the hill and hollered, 'That thing was coming right after me!'" His face was etched with silent laughter.

"It was lots of fun back then, and some of that work seemed just too much at times. We didn't have any proper tools, only what we could find. If you had a bolt as big as your arm to saw, you used a cold chisel and a hammer. Now you use a torch and have it done in a minute."

He donned a striped engineer's cap, rose from his rocker, and walked out to his garden behind the garage to pull turnips. "This garden keeps me busy. Got enough to supply most of the neighbors. Got peaches, apple, grapes, scuppernongs and muscadines, cherries, chestnuts, as well as all I grow every year," he said, standing up straight with his large railroad man's hands full of fresh produce. He cocked his head to one side as if to preach in that gravelly voice of his. "So if I live another year, I'll be out here working in this garden. Gotta keep working. Surely die if I didn't."

Ida Yelton

The Bluebird Cafe still looked as it must have looked thirty-eight years before. That's when Ida Yelton bought the place, and even before that she ran it for the Bluebird Ice Cream Company of Spartanburg. The modest little cafe, which might easily have been overlooked beside the Union Trust Company, was the last of the old places on the square in Forest City. Ida Yelton was one of a kind, too. She still called familiar female customers "Honey" and chatted in a neighborly fashion with her regulars about the weather, the family, or the way it used to be in the little ice cream parlor on the square.

"Law', I've dipped ice cream 'til it blistered my hands. Back before the war, they used to come in here and stand in lines for big five-cent cones of cream, and I'd dip down in there and stack it up. Why, most of them children are grandparents now, and lot of them come back here every once in a while. They say they just want to see if I'm still in here."

"That Bluebird Ice Cream had more butterfat than any of the others. They had eighteen flavors, too. Used real fruits to make the flavors. I had the only one in town. Oh, they'd stand in line for that cream.

"We sold milk shakes for a dime, all kinds of sundaes for a dime and banana splits for the same price, ten cents. We'd put a whole banana in one of those stainless steel trays with a little liner, put on three scoops of cream, and then add strawberry syrup, chocolate syrup, pineapples, black walnuts, and cherries. Law', a man came in here last week asking for a banana split, and, oh, it would cost me a dollar to make one the way we used to do it."

Now seventy-seven, she wore her grey hair back behind her head in a neat bun. She leaned comfortably on the counter while speaking, occasionally looking out the front window at Main Street. "I come in here about five-thirty or six in the morning and stay 'til about five-thirty every afternoon. My relatives say, 'Why don't you quit? You don't have to work.'

"'No, I don't,' I says. 'I don't have to work, but I feel better doing this than sitting there at the house worrying myself over everything.' I reckon I'd have been done and gone if I'd just have sat there after my husband died. After fifty-six years together you can imagine how that would feel to be left.

"My son, Horace, he has been awful good to me. He said, 'Mother, I want to tell you one thing. If you want to work, then you work. But if you don't want to work, then don't.' He helps me in here every Saturday when we're right busy. He really can step around this place."

A customer came in. Without moving from where she was standing, she called, "What for you, Honey?" and took the order.

The Bluebird was unashamedly basic. The interior was pale blue, with darker blue seats and benches, blue revolving stools, and a shoe-scarred pipe footrest. A blue wooden-bladed fan hung from the ceiling near the door. Two potted plants stood in the window, where they could catch the morning sun. The cigarette dispenser still displayed an ad for now-extinct Cavalier cigarettes. The counter supported several glass cracker jars and the long-used cash register, its keys now wearing thin. Pictures of two grandchildren and two great-grandchildren sat in frames on a shelf over the soft drink machine.

Ida washed her own dishes by hand and ordered and bought her hamburger meat from the local packing company. "It's got to be lean steak or else I take it back," she said, sitting in the back booth, making her patties by hand. "It's real meat. I sell an awful sight of hamburgers."

She had many regular customers, who showed up daily. "Some of them have been eating with me for forty years." Uncle Bud, a country radio

announcer and one of the regulars, climbed up
on one of the stools, said his howdies to Ida,
and asked for a cheeseburger and a glass of milk.
"Yup, she's been here a long time," he drawled,
as she placed one of her patties on the grill and
began pampering it with the blackened butcher
knife she used as a spatula. "She's only made
one mistake that I can remember," Uncle Bud
grinned. "I believe it was one of the girls who was
working for her at the time. Sent out a hot dog on
a takeout order and forgot to put the wiener in.

"But her cooking, now that's good eating.
With my stomach trouble, the only people's cooking I can eat is my wife's and Mrs. Yelton's." Ida
smiled at that and served the radio announcer
his burger. While she was working on another
cheeseburger with lettuce and tomato, Uncle Bud
continued, "Look at that—all the termater she's
putting on it. Some people slices a termater so
thin it only has one side. But she puts *termater*
on it."

Ida smiled again. "Well," she said, "if I'm
eating a tomato, I want to be able to taste it."

"It takes three hands to hold on to that hamburger," Uncle Bud laughed, paying his bill
and leaving.

She watched him go. "He's an Uncle Bud
all right. There's just one of him." And she set
about cleaning up, washing the one or two plates
that had accumulated from the morning. "I guess
I have been here a long time, but I've enjoyed
every minute of it. My greatest joy is talking to
people. And I really like people."

The Dycus Brothers

The white-haired brothers, one eighty and the other eighty-five, rocked in peaceful unison on the porch of their home just outside Ellenboro. "You know," mused C. O. Dycus to his brother, E. B., "a man gets up in years and begins to think back. You can see you've learned a lot that you didn't know when you were younger. Aw, we're just young bucks, but we've just learned how to get around. Just watch the world go by."

The two brothers were in the photography business back around 1910, when they scoured the Carolinas, seeking business. "We went from house to house, getting people's originals and having enlargements made of them," E. B. explained. "We'd ship them to Shelbyville, Indiana, where they'd make enlargements, sixteen by twenty, for fifty cents."

C. O. recalled, "We got ten dollars a week in the picture business, working in five states. When wages improved, I bought my father's farm, the place I was born and raised in, a log house they built up near Hopewell. I also bought a new Ford car for $335."

E. B. joined in, telling the story of the Ford T-Model, one of the first in the county. "We went up to Rutherfordton to get it off the flatcar. It came in a huge crate. Took us half the day to get it open. So we brought it home, and the next day we tried to start it so's we could learn how to run it. Well, it wouldn't hit a lick. They had told us to jack it up and try to start it in high. It just wouldn't do the trick. We called the man Pruitt that sold it to us and told him we don't want no car.

"Well, he came out there and looked the car over and said, 'Where's the switch key?' Well, I'll be darned if we hadn't left it in the house on the fireboard. Forgot all about it. Course it started right up with the key," E. B. laughed, sending the rocker back and forth on the battleship-grey front porch.

C. O.'s wife, Rose, produced an old picture of Arbor Day in Ellenboro in 1897. A large crowd of formally dressed villagers were massed around a long picnic table. An excursion train stood in the background. "That's back when they had Arbor Day," said C. O. "I believe I'm in that picture somewhere, because both of us, E. B. and I, we remember going to those things they had. J. P. D. Withrow would come down riding a mule and playing a mouth harp once a year, and they'd have tubs of lemonade, greased pig chases, and eatin', and cherry tree plantin'. They'd really make a day of it. Doc Bright used to donate the trees. Then in 1954 they cut the trees down. Got shed of 'em. They got too big I reckon. Got to be a nuisance."

The family used to own a mica mine. "It belonged to my grandfather," said E. B. "But I sold it in the Depression for three hundred and fifty dollars. Since then they've brought out ninety-two thousand dollars worth of micer. It was a good grade of micer, the best they ever found in the state. They'd haul it up to Spruce Pine to be processed. I mean they got the micer out of there. Only thing was, one man was killed up there. A man and his boy were digging and they found a vein. They cut into it and went too far, so it collapsed on them. The boy came running up to the house, pretty crippled himself, hollering that his dad was all covered up." E. B. let that story end and shifted into another tale.

"C. O., let's tell 'em about the time we tried selling those pictures to people working in the field." E. B. wagged his head in laughter. "Remember old Jack Johnson, the prize fighter? Well, we bought a bunch of his pictures for almost nothing and could sell them for four dollars apiece. Well, we spotted this bunch of workers,

so I went on out there and showed them the pictures and was taking orders just as fast as I could go with all them people crowding around, when up comes the man on a big black horse and him wearing a brown derby and carrying a big walking stick. I said to myself, 'Uh oh, I'm in the wrong place.' He looked down at me and said, 'Friend, by which road did you come in by?'

"I pointed to the nearest one and said, 'That one, sir.'

"And he said, very calmly, 'Then I suggest you get right back on it!' and I didn't question him at all but left in a hurry.

"But it worried me. We had about two hundred dollars business out there, so we slipped back at night and delivered those pictures and got

our money," E. B. finished up triumphantly.

That story led into another tall tale—about snake medicine. "Yes, it's a secret. I got the patent and everything, signed by all of them down there in Raleigh. It's made out of wild herbs. I think an Oklahoma Indian learned my daddy how. It was good stuff. Would cure up snakebites fast," E. B. said.

"A man down in the Shelby hospital was spider bit and had pneumonia as well. He heard about the Dycus snake medicine and sent his son up here for some. Well, the doctor, Doc Schenk, thought the old man was going to go that night, so it wouldn't hurt to try a last-ditch effort. The next day they sent for me, but they didn't tell me if the old man had lived or not. Well, I figured he had passed on and they were after me. That trip to Shelby was worse than a whipping. I got down there to the hospital and found his room. Well, if he wasn't sitting up in the bed, eating dinner. He saw me and grabbed me around the neck and got me down on the bed there, just a-cryin' and carrying on so. And in ten days he went home. Doctor Schenk told me later that he wished he had a couple more bottles of the stuff."

E. B. ended the story and took off on another one, about the time they loosened the wheels on his daddy's rig, so one wheel and then the next fell off as his father went riding down the road. "It makes me ashamed to think back on that and him such a sweet person and a minister as well.

"But I'll tell you one more story, about the biggest lie I ever told. I was twenty-five when I got married, and my little bride was just seventeen. Well, I said, that'll never do. It sounded too far apart, so when we went up there to get the marriage license I said that I was twenty-two and she was eighteen, just to put it closer together.

"Well, when it came time for me to go on Social Security, they discovered I really wasn't that old, or that young, so I admitted it, that fifty years ago I had fibbed about my age. They said, 'We're sorry, but you've lost three years of Social Security because of that lie.'

"Well, a time later I got to talking with Leonard Lowe about signing up for the Social Security. This was back when it was just starting, and we didn't know anything about it. He took me out to dinner down in Clemson, South Carolina, and we had a time. Then he said, 'Let's go back to my office and draw out the papers,' so we did and I said, 'How much will that be?' And he said, 'Five dollars.'

"Five dollars! and he had taken me to dinner and then sharped me out into signing that paper. I was so mad I almost drove off the road going home. But then, not so long after, I got a check from the Social Security for $1,103. It was the three years back Social Security. So I had to admit that Leonard was pretty sharp and that it didn't pay to lie about my age."

The men were silent for a time, their chairs creaking on the wooden planks of the shaded porch. "Yep," reflected C. O., looking his brother in the eye, where a crinkling smile could be seen, "they used to call us ramblers."

Grover McDaniel

"Lordamercy, people don't use mules no more. I 'bout quit the horse and mule business. My career has done been passed by. I just kind of stay here for a pastime," Grover McDaniel said, resting both hands on a worn cane. "They wouldn't let you put a mule barn up in the middle of town nowadays." He sat in the yawning mouth of the high-rafted building on Trade Street with the words "G. C. McDaniel, Horses and Mules Bought and Sold" emblazoned in white on black across the top. Along with friends Wilbur Smith and Henry Wells, Grover was watching the traffic, telling stories, discussing the weather, and talking about how things used to be.

In the mule business for sixty years, the eighty-six-year-old McDaniel had witnessed great changes in Southern farm life. "I've seen the day we've had a hundred and twenty-five head of mules in here. Used to have these barns full. Around World War I people used mules back then. Not anymore. Nobody much uses work animals. Just tractors. Oh there's just a few mules back up in the country."

"There's not a mule between the river and Marion," Henry added.

The men resting on their canes in the doorway were as much a part of the local landscape as were the barn's worn wide and sagging floorboards—grown dark and uneven through years of animal stamping—or the feeding troughs eroded in deep Vs from the constant rubbing of the necks of feeding horses and mules. The wide doors permitted light to enter and a breeze to flow through, making the barn "the coolest place in town in the summer," according to Wilbur.

Down at the far end of the barn a fifties model Chevy farm truck stood, its original color obscured by a heavy coat of dust. On the hood somebody had written "hot stuff." The pungent odors of hay and manure permeated the air. In the rafters families of sparrows chirruped about.

A rack of cracking leather mule harnesses and rusting trace chains hung limp and discolored, bent with weather and time.

The sun broke intermittently through the air vents and rafters, burnishing the hay into gold. The sole residents of the barn were a white mare and a bandy-legged foal. The mare impatiently stamped her hooves and whinnied to her newborn.

The trio of men sat in their chairs. Wilbur leaned one elbow on a turn-of-the-century school desk. The talk, as usual, was of the past.

"Oh, good gosh, I came here when I was twenty, back in '05, and there weren't but two stores here. George Horne's and the Biggerstaff stores. Kinda general merchandise places. I remember when it was called Burnt Chimney, but I can't tell you exactly why," Grover said.

Henry noted, "I remember the old well that was out front on Main Street with the big oaks around and roots out on the ground slick as a mole hole. I watered my horses there many a time."

Grover went on, "I remember those steer wagons that used to come out of Henderson, Buncombe counties, out of the mountains to sell with apples, chestnuts, cabbages, and the like. They'd be backed up a half a mile long like covered wagons.

"Lordamercy, there wasn't a wide place in the street. There wasn't lights, there wasn't nothing. After a good rain the streets were like mush, a big mud hole.

"I can't say it today, there once was a time when I knew all the country people well. You can imagine, they all dealt with me, or I was going out there to see what they had to swap."

"Yeh, this place is headquarters for all the old country farmers," Wilbur agreed.

"And it ain't what it used to be," Grover added. "There used to be people in here all the

time. That's why we started Second Monday, so many people come here to swap and trade things.

"Me and Fred Harrill started it around 1920, and Second Monday's still going strong. Never stopped from that first day. We got the old man at the *Courier* to run a little ad for us. What was his name? I just can't remember. Drove a little red mare in a buggy. I can see it now, but I can't remember his name," Grover said, scratching his forehead.

"But my Lordamercy, when we opened that first day, there must have been seventy-five mules tied out to the posts we'd put out there. There'd be one thousand people out there talking and swapping. And maybe they don't buy anything, but it's been good for the town and the county. Maybe they get acquainted and come back next week and buy something.

"I must say the town's been good to me. Always has been. I'll never stop braggin' on Forest City. We've got a good little town," Grover said.

The three men bent toward one another for

a farmers' joke about some slick dealing during a bull sale. They told their stories with the punchlines repeated for effect. An informal circle of friends, they tapped their shoes methodically, drummed their fingers on the old chair legs, and clinked their key chains, marking the passing time with their own inner rhythms.

"Used to go get a load of mules from Atlanta," Grover said. "It's right hard to get a mule nowadays. Over in East Tennessee they're still growin' 'em. Not many mules to be seen around here.

"A year ago I was selling a good many mules.

A year ago I was. Nothing beats a good horse or mule if you got a little garden. Soon be the day when it'll just be tractors," he trailed off, looking out the broad door to the parking lot, where the mules of trade day were once tied.

Conversation stopped. Wilbur peered thoughtfully over his cut-rim glasses at the clouds. Henry stared at the floor. Grover leaned his chin on his cane. And the whole thing began again. "Rain just may blow over this evening," Grover said softly.

Foy Biggerstaff

F. E. Biggerstaff's General Store in Sunshine was a treasure house for the browser, junker, and cracker-barrel philosopher, as well as for the person who wanted to find plow blades, lid lifters, ax handles, butter molds, chamber pots, and malaria tonic. From the ceiling, on top of the light fixtures, climbing the walls—everywhere—there was everything one could imagine.

"Why sure I got eight-inch lag bolts," responded the king of this wonderfully chaotic place. "Got railroad spikes, too." Foy Biggerstaff chomped on a cigar stub and surveyed his crowded shelves. "Well, I don't sometimes know where everything is. But when you get as old as I am, you don't give a damn anymore. Nettie here'll get for you."

Nettie Luckadoo had been working there for nineteen years. "That's too long, ain't it," she said, leading the way to the warehouse behind the store, where she remembered the lag bolts were.

"He won't tell you how old he is," she smiled briefly. "But he's seventy-something, because me 'n' him started school at Sunshine the same year."

Foy was one of the last of the old-time general store managers. It wasn't a very profitable venture anymore for him. "My oldest boy can make more money selling peanuts. I'm not makin' any money, I'm just gettin' by. That's what I'm doin'."

The Biggerstaff store had been in Sunshine for five generations, and that included some colorful history. As Foy told it, "My great grandfather was killed in a gun battle with robbers breaking in the store. I think he killed one or two of 'em before they got him." Foy returned from New York in 1939 to take over the store and had been there ever since. "Of course, I'd like to live another twenty years. But when I'm through with the store, I guess they'll just pile it all up and sell if for nothin'."

He walked slowly through the aisles waving at certain areas of merchandise marked with his

139

own humorous spellings. Here was a barrel with a sign "Sukkers, 2 for 1¢," and another box marked "Oddball closeouts, 10¢" or "Sopedish, 5¢." "Oh, it's just junky stuff," he said flatly. Then stopping by a crate of plow points, slings, and blades, he noted, "I don't sell plowing stuff but once in a blue moon," and then holding up a dusty box of safe dials, he said, "You don't sell one of them every day." He even had used underwater cameras and an emergency flare pistol.

Meanwhile in the back of the store the police monitor radio buzzed and crackled. Foy said that his main items of sale were kerosene lamps, cast-iron pots and pans, shoe tacks, and plumbing fixtures. "Country folks still need all those things," he said simply. Passing the grocery counter, he noted, "Don't have too many. Groceries aren't profitable nohow anymore."

Walking up to the front of the store, past the copper tubing, bedpans, butter molds, and pocket watches, Foy rested himself easily on one elbow by the freezer and pulled on the dimly pungent cigar.

Behind him piled neatly all the way to the ceiling in labeled cigar boxes was Foy's assortment of cure-alls. "There's something for warts — and for seasickness," he said. He pointed to another selection of old remedies, including the hard to find Hood's Compound of Gentian, Bitter Orange, and Sarsaparilla and Grove's Tasteless Chill Tonic for Malaria, or Chills and Fever. The country general store manager of old days needed a keen knowledge of herbs and medicines. Foy was one of the last to profess that knowledge. He even thought about going into medicine — as he said — "Back before I had any sense."

Things had changed drastically from the time when the general store was the hub of the community. "I have to have a little bit of everything still," he said, "just to get by. But now, things have changed so. I used to be able to sell dynamite, opium, and even marijuana," he said, displaying old North Carolina licenses for the sale of those items. "Sure," he explained, "Paragoric has opium in it. Now you have to go to the doctor for three bucks and then to the drug store for three more bucks to get what I used to be able to sell for twenty-five cents."

A couple of customers came in to shop, browse, and chat. Sitting on the ice cream freezer, one chided Foy. "Lookit that," he grinned at the clock. "Foy's not even turned his clock back to daylight savings time yet."

"By the time I get around to changing them, it'll be time to set it back to normal time," Foy joked back. "Besides, there're too many clocks around here to change. And I'm getting too old to change 'em."

Foy's store was blithely behind the times. It was a vestige of a time when the country general store was the repository of the spirit and soul of the community.

"That'll be eighteen cents for the lag bolts and fifteen cents for the lid-poppers," Foy computed out of the vacant side of his mouth. Accepting the cash, he bid the visitor a hearty goodbye. "Y'all come back when y' need some more oddball stuff."

Melvin Hoppes

To all but natives, Hoppes's mill was an unlikely sight in the village of Bostic. On the tin roof, grain dust had spewed from the top of the mill and formed a mat several inches deep, where grass and gangly sumac bushes had sprouted. Inside the weatherboard building great draping chandeliers of flowered cobwebs decorated the overhead rafters, and flour dust coated everything, including machinery, bags of feed, and the miller, Melvin Hoppes.

A cardboard sign on the front door advertised "Pigs for sale." The front door stood open regardless of the weather. A woodstove created a pocket of warmth in one corner, where a big cat snoozed in a chair.

Seventy-one-year-old Hoppes of Bostic warmed his hands at the woodstove. "I reckon I'll be a-sawin' wood on Christmas Day. Me 'n' my boys. I allus cut wood on Thanksgiving enough to get me to Christmas. Then I cut another load on Christmas Day to last me to spring."

By Advent, Hoppes was busy milling full time for farmers in the area. "Why, most folks come a-haulin' in their feed in here mostly in fall and winter," he said. "I didn't get home 'til after one-thirty none of the days, I've been so busy last week. People come from further and further away. Reckon it's 'cause this here is the only corn mill around. There ain't nary other one like it nearby. See, I do *your* meal here. Don't just give a man any cornmeal 'cept his own. New folks come every month inquirin' about my millin'. Folks from Gastony, Knoxville, Tennessee, b'low Chesnee, Lanc'ton."

Outside a winter drizzle tinkled on the mill's tin roof. Hoppes sank smiling into the chair by the stove and cradled the cat in the lap of his weathered overalls. His felt hat was covered with flour dust, giving it a ghostly look.

He laughed with a falsetto cackle and loosed an accurate stream of tobacco juice toward the waiting cinder bucket. "Cat's name is Mommy. Woman in Gilkey brought me that cat. I saw here she come with that cat in a wicker basket, and that was the start of it. Since then, I've had cats and kittens in here by the baskets." He indicated the wood box where two kittens idled happily.

"I've had as many as eighteen in here. Why, five hundred dollars wouldn't pay for all the cat food I've bought," he chuckled. "I give 'em away to boys and girls. Got shed of all of 'em now 'cept these three. Gave two of them to two old men up here from South Carolina who'd had heart attacks. They said, 'We would tend to a kitten,' so I gave 'em one each. I like to help other folks—and they help me. Besides, I know. I've got to have my cats," he grinned.

Putting the cat in her own chair, he got up to stoke the stove. "I give a dollar for it," he said, shoving a split oak piece into the open door of the stove. "I can't stay here without my fahr. My old stove give out last year, so I took me an old hogfeed liner and fixed it. I just study things out, and usually I can make it.

"I carpentered around here for years. I done everything myself. Couldn't get no hep. You can't hire no one to do nothin'. Built about twelve houses 'round here. Then I retired a whole week," he laughed. A gleam of good humor constantly played off his lined face. "I tol' my wife, I says, I got to get outa here. The four walls, they'll have me squeezed to death.

"I bought this place ten year ago from Wilbur Harrison. He ran it for twelve years. It was built back in the thirties by Johnny Hollifield, who built it for a planer shed. Then Old Man Dob Martin bought it. Then Sammy Gettys had it and put cows in here.

"I done a little bit of everything. You have to. That way, you don't have to take just any job. A man that can do lotsa things can do what he likes. I farmed, built houses, run this mill, and for five

143

year I welded invasion barges and victory ships at the Baltimore shipyard," Hoppes related.

That old-time skill of doing anything with your hands came to Hoppes out of necessity. His father died when he was eleven, and he "quit school in the fourth grade and come home to the farm and finished twenty acres of cotton. I had to. I was the oldest boy. I been workin' ever since. All it takes is good old common sense and mother wit. Yes, mother wit."

Hoppes opened the door on his woodstove and pushed in another log. "You can't fool me on corn," he said. "I can tell the moment a man comes in here with a big load what kind it is. I got two mills here. A hammer mill for feed and a corn mill for corn. Old-timey limbercob corn makes the best bread."

"Oh, man, he makes the best cornmeal you can put your mouth on," an old friend, Kent Lee, declared, waving his cane toward the miller.

Hoppes grinned and admitted, "I've ground a turn or two," dusting his cornmeal-covered hands on his faded overalls. He hoisted himself from the chair and poured a bag of corn in the top of the funnel and turned on the machine. With a whine, pulleys and gears meshed and rolled into life. Inside the faded red box, the millstone whirled, as the miller bent to engage the stones properly. With another turn of a handle the corn was let into the mill. The clamor of the machinery made talking difficult, and flour dust filled the air as a floury waterfall of cornmeal shot out the spout.

When the run was finished, Hoppes turned off the mill and took a handful and smelled it. Then he rolled some between his forefinger and thumb. "Ever had cornmeal mush?" he asked. "Now this'll make the best. This mill's the onliest one in the country like this, you'uns know that."

Hoppes bagged the "poke" of meal and tied it off carefully with cloth ribbon. He crossed his hands across his chest. "Yep, I'll be seeing my three young'uns again at Christmas and cuttin' one passle of fahr wood."

Rile Watts

Eighty-one-year-old rockmason Rile Watts hoisted the three-pound hammer high over his head and confidently brought it down hard on the head of the hand-held chisel. The visitor winced, thinking of that heavy hammer glancing off and hitting the hand. But to a man who had cut, shaped, and handled rock for most of his years, a miss was unthinkable.

"Lordamercy, I don't know any other rockmasons around, my age or much younger. Not many in the country left. Shore ain't. I guess I been working the rock seventy-some year." Watts was building the rock veneer finish on the last house he was ever to rock. "Don't advertise it," he grinned. "I reckon Bob's house here is see'd and talked about more'n any house I ever did."

He stood straight and strong backed in his faded green work pants and shirt, the latter buttoned customarily right to the collar, both now greyed with a fine mist of granite dust. He wore a colorless slouch hat pulled in low over his glasses. His hair too had grey color, matching the color of the rocks he worked with. And his eyes had their own sparkle, like tiny flecks of mica caught in the sun. His hands were rough and the whorls on his fingertips had long ago been worn down by the many rocks he had handled.

"I got started on walls first. I always like that. Then I was foreman in the WPA project building the old Hollis rock school. I had a bunch of no-counts workin' with me, so I did most of the work. After that I did the Polkville Methodist Church. And then a house over in the middle of Hendersonville. That's how I got commenced." He interspersed his talk with rock laying, both in the measured pace of his ages-old craft. Slowly, the unique pattern of rock on rock was covering the concrete-block retaining wall.

"I get this rock from around Table Rock up above Morganton. There's an old mountaineer up there. Shoots dynamite off and loads us up. The feller whose house this is has been haulin' his own rocks, and that's help.

"I have to split it up. Just use a hammer and a cold chisel. T'ain't no trouble. Oh, you strike one that won't give in now 'n' then. But I ain't struck one that I couldn't split in a good while."

Watts deftly manhandled a fair-sized rock in both hands and expertly carried it to its position with a minimum of wasted energy. "Folks want to know if the rocks get heavier as I get older, but I can't tell much difference." Then he added, "Does seem like the last twenty-five or thirty years have gone right fast though."

"Most fellers at eighty-some retires, dies, or sump'n. I just keep goin'." He grinned and placed the flat slab in its place. He tapped the rock gently with the butt of the hammer to adjust it into position, then measured the difference with dead-reckoning on the rock-hammer handle. "Got to cut it here, three inches out from the blocks," he told himself.

With a well-placed stroke he split the rock to the desired size. Then, trowel in hand, he dipped into the mortar and, with an easy flick, deposited the mortar in a neat column on the rock edge, a bit of artistry that belied its difficulty.

His hands for the most part stayed clear of the mortar—it ate the flesh. But he couldn't help touching the mix sometimes. It had stopped bothering him long before. "Oh, I've worn out my hands on occasion. But you get 'em tough

after awhile. I've had to tape 'em up, but now I don't pay 'em any attention."

The new rock was firmly in place. It fit snugly and it pleased him. Watts stood up, placed a foot high on the part of the wall yet to be rocked, and tipped back the felt hat as some sort of signal that it was break time.

He took a brief tour of the entire house to inspect the work. "This is what's called rock veneer. I'm just building over the woodwork of the entire house." He led the way through the family room to the massive downstairs rock fireplace, fully fourteen feet across. "A man could just take off his shoes and sit by the hearth here," he said.

Rock work like this was slow. Faced masonry was not like laying brick or block. Laying each

rock was a precarious gamble. Building with the rock face exposed, as opposed to flat-laid masonry, only one course—or, at the very most, two courses—could be laid at a time. And Watts insisted on taking his time and doing it right. "I'm all right as long as they give me time."

He liked to do other things as well—a little gardening for instance. "I do a right smart bit of truck farmin', too. Good crop of beans this year. I used to farm for a living.

"Shoot-fahr, I was in that *De*-pression. I guess you're too young for that. I was in that thing head over heels. Picked cotton when it was goin' for ten cents a pound." He lowered his voice. "I'll never go that way again."

Strangely enough, Watts never built a house out of rock for himself. "I thought I would some-time, but I stay busy helping the other feller. But if I ever do, hit'll be out of that Cherry Mountain rock. He won't split. Got to use him as he is— that Cherry Mountain rock."

Home-owner Robert Toney was watching as Rile went back to heaving rocks around like chair cushions. "I'll tell you," confided Robert. "I helped him one day, and he can work me down. And that's a fact."

Overhearing this, Watts let his face go into a many-seamed grin. "I guess I'm pretty active to be going on eighty-one, but I'll have to admit, I do have to slow down now going up hills."

149

Soapmaking at the Murphys'

"This here soap receipt is over one hundred years old," said Edna Murphy. "Got it from his (indicating Ernest sitting nearby in the shade) older aunt. And she was eighty-three years old when she died." Over an open fire in the back-yard Edna slowly stirred an ancient black cast-iron pot, which she claimed was nearly as old as the recipe. One of Ernest's richly grained hickory ax handles made a fine paddle.

It was a perfect day for making soap—not too windy, not too hot or dry. The sun was blazing away, burning off blackberry winter's last frost. The fire produced a delicious aroma, making the bubbling soap appear almost edible. In fact the goo had the color and consistency of Thanksgiving turkey gravy.

Ernest cackled at the thought of eating the stuff. "You drink a pint of that and it might kill you. I don't know, but it might kill you."

It had been two years since Edna last made her soap. "Last year I didn't need any and I just, well, had too much to do."

She had earlier put the twenty-two quarts of water and two cans of Red Devil Lye in the pot to heat. Edna recalled that the authentic old-time way of making soap dictated getting the lye from the fireplace ashes or woodstove hopper. "That's the way my mother used to do it," she said.

Making soap reminded her of a tragic piece of family history. Slowly stirring the mixture, Edna recollected, "I was seven or eight at the time when my mother took the fever. The whippoor-wills had gathered 'round the hopper and hollered right before that, and we took that as a warning. Not long atter that, she died."

Just then the wind blew a leaf into the pot, and

Edna exclaimed, "Why, there's a leaf in here."

Ernest just grinned, "Aw, leaves is awright."

Back to her task, Edna added what she called in her recipe "bucket grease." That was drippings she had saved over the years from "old pure hog lard I've set back."

She brought this to a boil and cooked it until it thickened, while watching the heat. "If you have too much fahr, hit'll boil over," she warned.

Keeping Edna company with a constant stream of teasing ("Yer messin' up. The worst I ever saw."), Ernest supervised the fire.

She finally held up the hickory stick and watched with satisfaction as the light brown liquid "threaded" off the bottom of the stick. "Jus' like makin' 'lasses," Ernest advised. At last the turpentine and ammonia was added. This, Edna instructed, was to "keep flies and worms away from the soap." When the mixture was cooked to her liking, she began ladling it out of the pot into a large wash tub, to cool and solidify overnight.

The next afternoon, she and Ernest carried the washtub to a nearby work table and dumped it upside down. The cake of soap ("lookin' just like the bottom layer of a wedding cake") plopped out on the open feed sack that had been spread on the table.

With a large butcher knife, she began slicing the cake—until Ernest could stand it no longer and insisted he do the carving. The soap was soft and pliable, not yet fully stiff. Its color had lightened from beige to that of mutton fat.

The cutting job done, they stood back proudly to survey their work. On another table, Edna placed individual blocks of soap to dry further. She used it to wash clothes with, cutting half of one cake into slivers in her washing machine each time she did a load of clothes. Holding up one such cake, Edna said with surety, "I'll tell you, this soap'll clean clothes better'n that stuff you buy." And Ernest chimed in, "Yeh!"

153

Planting by the Signs

"Mostly when I go to planting," Hoyle Greene advised over the top of his round wire-rim glasses, "I look at this here almanac. Then I just sit back and watch it grow," he giggled. "Hee-hee, I just sit back and watch it grow."

Hoyle recovered himself and explained, "There's a good deal of people in town who don't go by the signs, but that's nothing to me. They don't have nothin' but a little piece of a garden. But I want to know what I'm a-gettin'. You go by this almanac and you'll come out on top."

Greene had been gardening, he said, since he was ten. About signs, he said, "I've been caught a time or two by not payin' attention. Planted beans when the signs was in Virginia," as he referred to Virgo, "and them beans were all flower and stalk. You see here," he said, pointing to his copy of Blum's Almanac. "When the gal there is holding them blossoms, then stay out of the plantin' business.

"I recall once't I planted a row of half-runners and didn't look at the signs. Then I saw what I'd done, waited a day, and planted two more rows. Well, the sign had changed, and that first row piddled around and gave me a bean here and a bean yonder. One here, one yonder. While, on the other hand, them there two rows was just loaded down."

Sitting in a chair beneath his faithful cider apple tree, Greene thumbed through his almanac to the table for March. "See here, today's in that there Virginia. It'd be a good day for plowing but that's all. Wait 'til Saturday when the sign's right.

"You gotta watch the moon. The almanac here tells you all about it. Plant corn by the full of the moon, lots of folks say. Or plant corn when you hear the doves first call in the spring. Some old people go on that. And then some say to plant corn when the blackberry vines bloom.

"Me, I planted two rows of cabbage last week by the signs. Went down to the ice plant at the feed house that Ol' Man Heffner's got there and asked for cabbage that'd make great big ol' heads. Then I came home and dug a couple of holes 'bout wrist deep in the garden to see if it was dry enough to plow. I waited 'til Saturday morning, and I saw the soil would do right. The soil didn't stick to the digger, so I got out my Merry Tiller—I call her my 'Merry Go Round'—and I went to plowin'. The next mornin' about six o'clock I saw that the full red moon was goin' slam down behind Sweezy Mountain, and I knew it was time to plant," he grinned proudly. "Expect to have a real good garden this year."

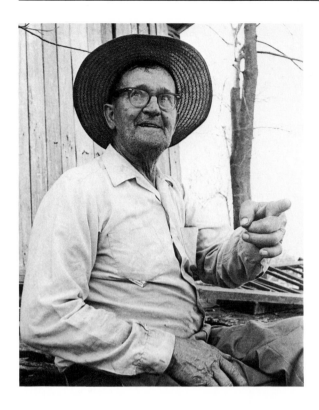

The Murphys also watched the phases of the moon at planting time. "We go by the moon, y'know," Ernest intoned. "Getcha a Birthday almanac and hit'll larn you all about it. For instance, we kill and cure our own meat. Y'only kill on the going down of the moon—before the moon news. If the meat swells up in the pan and the grease don't run out, then hit was kilt in the wrong time.

"And you cut wood on the new of the moon, or else hit'll sob. Not dry properly. Or else hit'll have blue streaks in it."

Edna told the story of Ernest's famous hernia operation in February—famous because Ernest came back from the hospital and walked the footbridge with no trouble. "Ernest went down to the hospital, and the doctor told him he was too busy and couldn't do the operation until next week. Well, Ernest told him, 'Well, I'm glad of it, for the moon ain't right.' The next week the signs were down in the legs right where Ernest wanted them, and everything went perfect like."

Spurge Freeman of Pea Ridge was out plowing with "community dog" Tony running beside the old Farmall 200 as it steadily turned the red soil.

"You can't go by the doves this year," he said, shoving his hat back and wiping his brow, "They've gone to hollering too soon—heard them way last month. The whole world's got turned around. It's been one of the most unusual winters I've seen in my seventy-five years."

Freeman said he didn't go by the signs too much. He planted his Irish potatoes because it was the right time of year. But he conceded that he watched the moon, explaining, "The full moon might' near regulates the earth, don't you think so?"

Greene advised that the three most productive signs, in order of productivity, were Cancer (signs in the breast), Scorpio (the "secrets" as the almanac bashfully called it), and Pisces (in the feet). He summed up, "You can guess at it, but that won't work very well. Getcha a Blum Almanac—or an ol' Birthday yallerback—and you can't go wrong."

There were other signs to go by. Some folks adhered to nature signs such as doves calling and, as Greene mentioned, blackberry vines blooming. But the strongest sign appeared to be the moon. J. T. Mayse of Pea Ridge said he didn't go much for other signs, but paid attention to the moon when it came to planting corn. "Plant corn by the full of the moon," he advised. "Some people says they's nothing to planting corn by the moon, but I know there are."

Down the road from Freeman lived Jessie Mace, a bright-eyed seventy-five-year-old gardener with the master touch. His little house off Pea Ridge was an island in a sea of turned soil.

"Well, I'll tell you, Son," Jessie began, clapping the visitor on the shoulder, "I been farmin' since I was six years old when my mother cut off a little hoe handle and put me out in front of her in the field. I thought it'd kill me, but she cut off a little hick'ry switch and stuck it there in her apron—and looked like she'd use it. So I lived through it. Twelve hours of hoeing. That's working.

"Now, let's go out here and lookit things." He paraded through the rows with measured giant steps. "Whattaya think that is?" he quizzed the visitor. "Naw, it's not kale. It's flowers. What kinda flowers is them, Fanny?" he hollered back

at the house. "Sweet willy-yam!" came his wife's response.

"And here's some old-timey poppies. When they bloom they'll knock your peepers clean out, Son." He strided toward the onion patch with the dog Brownie ("Hunts anything that moves in the woods.") close behind.

"Yes, I go by the signs. I've learned that they were perfect. It's true. Every word of it. The head, shoulders, arms, and feet are the best. Head and shoulders for Irish 'taters, corn in the arms. And feet are good for 'taters, too. Then when your corn is knee high, plant you some cornfield beans in between, but still pay attention to the signs.

"You gotta go by them signs, if you want a decent garden. If you plant Irish 'taters today you'll get nothing but 'taters full of little knots and

157

all strung out. Wait 'til Monday. The signs'll be right Monday for 'tater plantin'."

Jessie led around the house, digging up "old-timey onions" he pronounced Sherlock onions. Between stoopings to grasp the onions by their greens, he advised, "If you plant corn when the sign is Virgo, it'll just wind around in the ground and you won't get even half a stand."

Jessie noted that the doves weren't reliable anymore, as they "go to hollering all winter. You can't hardly go by that anymore. Of course it used to be that when doves hollered that meant spring had broke."

Jessie explained about several other nature signs he used. A rain sign he depended on came from cloud formations. "You see up there those streaky clouds," Jessie said, pointing to the west, "where it looks like a mare's tail throw'd up. Well, that's a sign for rain.

"And I go by the stars, too, but you'd have to come back at night for me to show you about that," he grinned. "And the closest star to the moon is a sign. It's sorta complicated, but nine times out of ten, if it's on the south side, it means rain, and if it's on the north, it means clear and windy."

Jessie sat slowly in the shade behind the garage barn. "That there's a new garden I've turned. I've just laid around here and haven't put in my English peas like I oughta have." He took off a massive straw cowboy hat to reveal thick black hair lightly laced with silver.

"Betcha don't learn this sorta stuff in college," he laughed. "Well, you should. This here is just learnin' how to get along in the world with nature.

"Come back any time and I'll teach you all that old-timey stuff." Then he stopped, peered at his henhouse, and ventured, "Don't want a rooster, do ya? Got five and can't get shed of them all."

Old-time Christmas

Old-time Christmas in the Carolina hill country was a reflection of the times—lean but joyful—full of a very special excitement born of isolation and simplicity.

Aunt Abe Brown remembered Christmas as one of eight children in the family log cabin in Green River Community. It was a very special time for the Abrams clan. "Mama always told us two or three weeks before Christmas that if we were real smart then Santy Claus would come to see us. And so we didn't have to be told to get firewood, sweep the floor, nor gather the turnips for friends who didn't have as much.

"We would gather holly with beautiful berries and decorate the mantel from the floor plum up to the top with greens and pin berries and leaves that wasn't frostbit on the curtains.

"We didn't have a tree until my brothers came back from a visit to some wealthier folks' place, and we started the idea too. We got a little holly bush and just strung popcorn around it. But most folks don't have Christmas trees in the country.

"We'd hang our stockings and all go off to bed. We had our beds on the other side of the partition in the log cabin. Dad would take the poker outside the house and scrape it along the back of the chimney," Aunt Abe laughed. "Bob could always hear Santy Claus.

"We'd get a little doll, maybe. One with a china head, arms, and legs. Their bodies and upper legs were stuffed with sawdust. I wish I had mine now. And maybe two or three little pieces of what was called 'tub candy' and some 'long tom' chewing gum. The boys might get a little bird whistle or a pistol."

The family always had a big Christmas dinner, with the mother cooking in the log kitchen, separated from the main log room by the traditional breezeway. "Sugar was scarce back then, we used molasses. We'd make gingercake. But we could usually save up enough sugar to bake a white coconut cake. My, we thought we were pretty wealthy to have a white coconut cake. We'd always have a big fat hen. And dressing too. We didn't have cranberry sauce, for we didn't know about cranberries. We'd have candied apples and candied sweet potatoes and always turnips."

Normally in the summer the eight Abrams children took their baths in the creek below the house. But getting spiffed up for Christmas required "taking our baths in a big ol' washtub in the kitchen beside a rip-roaring fire."

Children got one pair of shoes a year, and that was part of Christmas for Aunt Abe. "We'd go barefoot in the summer, wear our old shoes all spring and fall, and get a new pair every Christmas."

Aunt Abe recalled something her father used to say. "We didn't have much of this world's goods, but we shared what we had with love."

Hoyle Greene remembered Christmastime down on Big Island Road as being lean. "There wudn't nuthin' to give, ner nothin' to get. Just sat 'round the fire and cracked nuts." But he fondly remembered "big oak wood on the dog-arns and us kids a-crackin' them hick'ry nuts an' walnuts."

Christmas for the Greene children, Martin,

Otto, Mary, Elsie, and Hoyle, consisted mainly of hanging their stockings over the fireplace Christmas Eve and looking forward to "a stick of candy or chewin' gum."

"I remember one Christmas morning when somebody'd filled up the stocking with wood chips as big as your fist. I thought I had something," Greene grinned behind his black-rim, round glasses. "But it was in the family, so it didn't matter. Nope, never found out who did it."

At Piney Ridge School the teacher, Kate Gold, would "call each of us to the front of the room, and we'd each get a stick of candy, peppermint or stick kind.

"We'd all go rabbit hunting on Christmas Day. Neighbors'd gather at our place, and we'd go out. I towed many a sack of them ol' stiff rabbits on my back."

Customs of Christmas were spare back at the turn of the century. With chores such as splitting rails, hauling cordwood, and farming to occupy their time, many people just didn't have time, money, or inclination for decorations. "I never did hear tell of folks decoratin' 'til recently," Greene said, regarding the lights of Main Street in Forest City, "an' look where we are now. We never had a tree or nothin'. Talk about comin' up the hard way. Why young people now don't know what hard times there was way back yonder."

About old-time Christmases, Aunt Nan Harrill whooped, "Oh, Lordamercy, man, I think it's gone. We'd just hang up our stockings, but didn't get much but some candy or apple or something or other, maybe some peppermint candy as long as your forearm."

Raised on Piney Ridge as one of eight children, Nannie recollected best when she was older around Christmastime. "I'd get my banjer and go

162

over and sit by the fire and make me a cigarette and smoke and play after Mom and Dad had gone to bed.

"I never did care nothin' about dolls. I was too busy being outside with the dogs, stock, and cats. I didn't care for dolls. I was always out—out huntin' rabbits. I remember old folks would gang up together around the fire and tell tales and sech. There were to-dos and lots of parties. Folks'd cut up a little bit at Christmas."

Celestia Blanton, who lived with Aunt Nan, added, "My mother made me a rag doll once. And I got a china doll another time—with painted hair. I always wanted a doll with real hair. I had a little tree—a small Christmas cedar about a foot tall—and I dampened it and sprinkled it with flour to make it look like snow.

"And I'd always get up before sunup on Christmas and it'd be cold. The fire'd gone out. I always wondered how Santy Claus got down the chimney without getting his face black. So one Christmas Eve I peeked—and found out," she grinned mischievously.

Christmas for John Johnson meant more square dances. So when the boys came around the house getting ready to go play for a dance, John remembered his father grumbling, "Saul's troubled, Saul's troubled."

John laughed. "He didn't think much of my music. He wanted me to work there on the farm. But we'd light out, walking all the way down Pea Ridge Road of a night and every pothole filled with ice in the road. Play for a square dance 'til one o'clock or so and then I'd walk all the way back and have to slip into the house. Then Dad'd say at four o'clock, 'Let's get up and go to work. If you can play music then you can work.'"

Banjo picker John Johnson began playing for

164

dances when he was around sixteen. "Every night or two around Christmas there'd be square dances in people's homes. They clean out a big room that had a fireplace in it. The caller'd be there and we'd get in a corner and go at it with cross to yer partner and do-se-do with regular peppy dance pieces like 'She'll Be Comin' 'Round the Mountain' and 'Turkey in the Straw.' "

John was born in a log cabin in the Lincoln Hill section between Bostic and Washburn's Store. "I was born within sight of the house I'm satisfied Abraham Lincoln was a-born in," asserted John.

He remembered that in the winter the race along the millpond froze and "there was icicles as big 'round as I am hanging there from where the water was constantly trickling down. Back then Christmas was something we looked forwards to from way back in the summertime. We's warned that Santy Claus would be around if we were good. So we'd go gather holly in the woods, and Mother would decorate the house.

"Well, when Christmas Eve night rolled around, we were told to retire. I can remember just as plain as can be, not being able to go to sleep and then waking up in the morning. Boy, that was a thrill, in our stockings would be an apple and an orange and maybe a morsel of candy. No toys, no nothin' to throw down.

"Back then times was tough. They didn't buy toys for kids to throw out at the edge of the woods. But in a way I'd love to live some of those days again."

For Charles and Nannie Self, who lived in the mountains of the Golden Valley Community, Christmas meant baking and candy making. Nannie's Christmas baking on the waxed and fire-pitted Home Comfort filled the house with the spicy aromas of cinnamon, apples, and ginger.

The grey and silver woodstove dominated the kitchen with its warmth and charm. "I can re-

member the day my daddy bought that stove just as clear as if I's standin' there now. Hit was August of nineteen and twenty-four," declared Nannie Self. "A dealer hauled it up here with a mule and buggy.

"Lots of times just before Christmas I like to bake six pies at a time. The woodstove oven's so big you can do that. Well, that's really nice for in just three runs you'll have all you'll want. I just slip 'em in the freezer for later.

"Hit's hottest here over the fahr-box and cooler over here on the right side. Do the jelly on the right side and cannin' things over the fahr-box on the left."

Bun-warmers were overhead and fruit-drying drawer was under the oven itself. The Home Comfort had three fire-control devices: a draft-control damper in the stovepipe to keep the fire for a long time, another damper to reroute the warmth around the oven, and a sliding grate in the front to regulate air flow beneath the fire.

Nannie started her fire with corn-cobs soaked in kerosene, then fired the stove with wood brought in by her son Clayton, who lived just over on the next knob. She kept the stove "oiled" with parafin or beeswax, which kept the Home Comfort from rusting.

One old-time recipe that Nannie recalled was apple cake. Her father, Dan Melton, loved the stuff. "His birthday was the twenty-fourth day of December, and he'd always want a piece of that fruitcake. Hit was made with ten to fifteen layers of pancake-thin layers with dried apples cooked in between. Whoowee! He'd rather have that than anything."

The big stove dispensed candies, cakes, and cookies that country children saw only once a year. "Back then we thought Christmas would never come," Nannie laughed at herself. "Now, it's so that you can't even get your present bought in between Christmases. We were—folks were— one hundred percent happier back then at Christmastime. You were happier with less. Now folks want too much. Back then oranges and store candy was Christmastime stuff. Now, it's three hundred and sixty-five days a year. They enjoyed Christmas back then more because folks knew what it meant to go without. Then when they got something special, it really was special to them.

"Back then you didn't see nothing but stick candy, from the store. And they was big sticks like fat ol' candycanes. Well, we didn't see that store candy much. We made peanut candy and molassy candy. Charles used to make a world of molassy every year.

"With all that candy, cookies, and a-bakin' no wonder we kids used to think Christmas was something. And you got just one thing for a present. I remember the time I got a pair of gloves. That's all I got. And I thought that was the finest thing, for I had to walk four miles over to school at South Mountain Institute, and we were always given something that we needed. I thought I was something in those gloves, a-walkin' to school."

Charles volunteered, "I recollect one time my father gave me a little black-faced watch. I thought that was the best thing in the world. I tied it on a little string and stuck it in the watch pocket on my overhauls. Then one day after Christmas we were burning stumps, and I tossed one in the fire hit caught that string and jerked the watch into the fire. I thought I was rurnt then. I'll never forget that feeling. Hit didn't cost but a dollar, but I was rurnt."

Nannie smiled self-consciously. "December is my favorite month of all." Glancing across the room at snowy-crowned Charles, she said, "We were married in December."

"Why, hit was a wonderful time, Christmas was," grinned Quintenna Boone Hampton, of Green Hill, remembering her early Christmases deep in the high mountains of Madison County. "What we got, we's just as proud of as we could be. We just hung up our stockings around the mantel and would get candy and cookies, apples and oranges, and stuff like that. Hit was a wonderful time when Santy Claus came."

Children got precious little save special foods and fruits. Sometimes, Quintenna said, "maybe people who's lucky enough to be able to buy 'em would get dolls. Maybe a girl would get a handmade shuck doll."

Observing the difference between then and now, she asserted that if children of today awoke on Christmas morning to find only a well-filled stocking, "why, they wouldn't have no Christmas at all, would they? They can't get enough, it seems like. Hit ain't a bit like it used to be. Not a bit."

166

The eight Boone children shared the community Christmas at the church, but, like other mountain and country families, had no tree in their own home. "They had this big ol' tree in the church, and I remember havin' singin's and trimmin' the tree—all kinds of carryin' on. An' everybody went y'know. The men'd climb up there and jump out of the tree, slide off the branches to entertain the children, y'know.

"I remember the time seventy-four years ago we went for a big Christmas dinner at Bert Callahan's. They was a hog's head on the table with an apple in its mouth," she laughed. "Oh, we looked forwards to Christmas so. Hit seems like hit took forever. But now hit's like hit's Christmas for these children might' near every day.

"Lordee, folks don't know nothin' about Christmas no more."